F

JUBA THIS ✸✸✸ AND ✸✸✸ JUBA THAT

100 AFRICAN-AMERICAN GAMES FOR CHILDREN

Dr. Darlene Powell Hopson
and Dr. Derek S. Hopson
with Thomas Clavin

A FIRESIDE BOOK
PUBLISHED BY SIMON & SCHUSTER
NEW YORK LONDON TORONTO SYDNEY TOKYO SINGAPORE

FIRESIDE
Rockefeller Center
1230 Avenue of the Americas
New York, New York 10020

FIRESIDE and colophon are registered trademarks
of Simon & Schuster Inc.

Designed & illustrated by Jill Weber

Manufactured in the United States of America

10 9 8 7 6 5 4 3 2 1

Library of Congress Cataloging-in-Publication Data

Hopson, Darlene Powell.
Juba this and juba that : 100 African-American games for children / by Darlene
Powell Hopson & Derek S. Hopson with Thomas Clavin.
    p.   cm.
"A Fireside book."
Includes index.
1. Games – Africa. 2. Board games – Africa. 3. Handicraft – Africa.
4. Musical recreations – Africa.   I. Hopson, Derek S.   II. Clavin, Thomas.
III. Title.
GV1204.82.H66 1996
793'.096–dc20
                                                                95-25029
                                                                  CIP

ISBN 0-684-80781-5

THIS BOOK IS FOR ALL CHILDREN WHO ENJOY GAMES AND learning about people in other countries. May they discover that the world is full of playmates much like them.

We have found such children in our own homes: Dotteanna Hopson, Derek S. Hopson Jr., Kathryn Clavin, and Brendan Clavin. Let's continue to play and learn together.

We also dedicate this book to the nieces, nephews, and godchildren who teach us something new every day: Miles Byers, Odell Quan Harrington, Tiffany Harrington, Kenneth Douglas Hopson, Lamar Hopson, Teachon Milburn, Alyce Powell, Deanna Powell, Kelly Powell, Robert L. Powell III, Sharena Powell, Ashley Scarletta, and Damano Scarletta.

Okay, all of you, have fun!

ACKNOWLEDGMENTS ✵

MANY PEOPLE DIRECTLY AND INDIRECTLY CONTRIBUTED TO the writing of this book. Foremost is our editor, Betsy Radin, who conceived it, had faith that we could do it, and offered encouragement along the way.

Another is Pamela Gwathney, our dear sister-friend who taught us a great deal about early childhood development and who celebrated the virtues of Kwanzaa before most people knew about this holiday.

We also want to thank those who have previously written about African games and their importance to a variety of cultures. This book could not have been written without a wealth of source material, much of it provided by libraries, particularly the John Jermain Library. Some of the authors are mentioned in the text, and to the rest of them we offer deep appreciation.

Last, but certainly not least, we thank in advance the parents, grandparents, teachers, and other caregivers of any racial and ethnic background who will use this book as an opportunity to play and learn with children.

CONTENTS ✲✲✲

Indoor Games   61

Board Games   82

Craft-Making Activities   101

Musical Games 119

Kwanzaa 140

Index 154

FOREWORD ✳✳✳

My favorite times are when my mom, my dad, my little brother, and I play games. I love when we play games from Africa. They are fun and make me feel proud. All of my friends like them, not just my black friends but my white friends too.

Everybody can have fun playing them. Sometimes we sing songs while we are driving in the car, especially when we go on long trips like visiting my grandparents. My brother, Derek Jr., is only two, so he doesn't know the words, but he tries to sing along anyway.

We celebrate Kwanzaa every year, and when my friends come over they learn about African-American traditions. Kwanzaa can be celebrated at school too!

I know you will have lots of fun playing and learning about games and activities from Africa. The best part is that everybody can play and sing together. Maybe one day I can play one of the games with you and your children!

My grandparents traveled to Africa and brought back gifts for me. I would like to save my money and travel to Africa one day.

Harambee,
Dotteanna Karyn Hopson
Age 8

INTRODUCTION ✸✸✸

The search by African Americans for roots in African culture is not new. It is part of a yearning that has existed for centuries. Whether they came to America as slaves or immigrants, African Americans have looked to their continent of origin as part of an effort to establish or foster identity and pride in their culture.

It may be misleading to say there is an "African culture." From Egypt to South Africa and from Ethiopia to Senegal, there are countries that have their own unique culture unlike those of their neighbors. Certainly there are common or similar traditions, beliefs, and practices. But there really isn't one specific, unified culture that defines the entire continent.

That's one reason for this book, to show the variety of African cultures that exist. That's also the reason why it's titled *Juba This and Juba That*. The word *juba* may have originated in West Africa, but most information available indicates that *juba* was used to describe food, or more specifically a meal eaten by nineteenth-century African Americans that included whatever items were available. "Juba this and juba that" meant putting into the same pot whatever was around to eat – leftovers from previous meals, sometimes combined with contributed items from neighbors or guests – and the family shared the result for lunch or supper. In a sense, however different or traditional the ingredients were, every dish of juba was new. We've taken a little of this and a little of that to cook up a book that shows the varied ingredients, or games, of African cultures.

Another reason for *Juba This and Juba That* is for readers to have fun. Haven't we all played games? Okay, some of us more than others – circumstances in some childhoods meant less time or encouragement for games, while for some people games have continued to be part of their lives no matter how old they became. But for most of us, no matter how hard we've worked or how many responsibilities we have, playing games is an ideal, something we wish we could do more or hope to do in the future or something we want to be a part of our children's childhood.

What hasn't been brought together before in one book are games that originated in Africa. Especially in recent years, there has been much scholarly study of what ideas, concepts, traditions, practices, knowledge, and influences have traveled from Africa to America. Games have not necessarily been overlooked, but they haven't been emphasized as an important component of African-American culture.

Games that originated in Africa are remarkable and probably haven't been given the full credit they deserve. In many communities there is little if any awareness that even the simplest games, enjoyed by children of any color, were developed in Africa – within villages, cities, societies, and tribes. The intention of this book was not to attempt to make up for any oversights, but it *was* to promote an understanding (or a deeper one) that a lot of the fun we do or can experience today emanates from African cultures.

Not every game in this book was first played in Africa or exclusively originated there. A game "invented" in, say, Nigeria could have been independently "invented" in India or Spain or by a Native American tribe. As we learn more, we're discovering how rich and varied cultures all over the world were and are. Also included here are games that may have originated elsewhere but evolved in Africa into the versions we are familiar with today.

Is this book strictly for African Americans? In one way, yes. Families seeking to enhance pride in their racial background can use this book as an example of the many wonderful activities and concepts Africa has produced. There may well be a special feeling when playing a game that originated or was developed by African ancestors. It is "ours."

But we hope people of any race or cultural background will enjoy this book. It is meant to be shared. Given that most children learn about each other on the playground, having youngsters of any racial or ethnic group play together is a great learning tool . . . and fun. People of Caucasian, Asian, and Latino descent are going to learn a lot about Africa from this book, and we hope they will appreciate what's different and similar among us.

It's true that one purpose of this book is that it be an educational tool. Parents, teachers, and caregivers can use it to supplement presentations about African cultures. But the foremost purpose is that the book inspire play. As psychologists – and more important, as parents – we realize that much of what is positive in the lives of our children comes from playing – social skills, physical fitness, a sense of fairness, and sharing moments that result in fond memories.

Go ahead, have fun . . . and maybe gain some surprising knowledge along the way.

Darlene Powell Hopson and Derek Hopson

OUTDOOR GAMES

Africa is a large continent, so the climate of a country in the west may not be the same as that of another country in the south, and the same is true for east and north. Certainly this is true of North America, where on a typical mid-October day the weather in Toronto, Canada, will probably be different from the weather in Mexico City.

Because of the oceans and the wind patterns, however, for most of Africa the climate is usually dry and warm. For this reason, over the centuries the people of Africa developed many outdoor activities and games, and these outdoor games have been handed down from generation to generation.

Also, in many African villages, child care was a community responsibility. As men and women worked in fields, developed inventions, and explored medicine and science, their children were supervised by groups of parents and relatives. The combination of open space, climate, and a large number of youngsters led to developing games that included a lot of physical activity for as many as three dozen players.

AMBUTAN

Number of Players: 6 to 8
Age: 8 to 12
Equipment: A stick or short pole

ORIGIN:

This game originated in Nigeria. It combines dexterity with judgment.

HOW TO PLAY:

1. A mound of sand or dirt is created and the stick is thrust into the middle of it.

2. The players sit surrounding the mound. Talking or singing a favorite song, they take turns gradually removing handfuls of sand from the mound.

3. As the mound diminishes, players have to be more careful, eventually using fingers to remove sand. The player whose "excavation" causes the stick to fall is out. The stick is returned and the players continue.

4. The game ends when only one player is left. If the game is played again, that player could be the one who scoops first each time during that game.

AMPE

Number of Players: 10 to 12
Age: 8 to 12
Equipment: None

ORIGIN:

This game was played by children in Ghana, and it helped them to gain coordination and agility.

HOW TO PLAY:

1. One player is chosen as the "leader," and the others stand in a semicircle, with the leader facing the player at either end of the group.

2. The leader and the player both clap hands. Then they jump in place at the same time. Then they jump and thrust one foot forward.

3. If the two have put the same foot forward, the leader is out and the player takes her place. If they have thrust different feet forward, the leader moves to the next player and the same routine begins.

4. A point is scored every time the leader is successful. Every player takes a turn as leader. The one who scores the most points wins.

ANIMAL KEEPERS

Number of Players: 6 to 10
Age: 6 to 8
Equipment: Sticky labels (or cards with tape)
Magic Markers

ORIGIN:

The Kikuyu tribe of Kenya is credited with developing this game. It is based on a myth that when the Kikuyu were first created, they were given a choice by the gods of a spear, bow, or digging stick. They chose the stick and became very good at farming. As time went on, they encountered many animals and birds and named each one based on its characteristics — and that's why the animals of Kenya have their names today.

HOW TO PLAY:

1. As many animal names are chosen as there are players. One player, the Keeper, does not participate. She writes the names of animals on the labels and sticks one on the back of each player.

2. The players wander around a small open field. They tap each other on the shoulder and offer one hint as to the animal's identity. For example, one player says to another, "You have tusks." If the player guesses "Elephant" and is correct, the label goes on his chest. If he's incorrect (guesses a different animal), the player who gave the hint moves on to the next player.

3. The object is for all of the "animals" to identify themselves correctly. A new Keeper is chosen and the game begins again, with players switching animals or the Keeper choosing new ones to go around.

ATAKLUI DADA

Number of Players: 2 to 4
Age: 8 to 12
Equipment: Black marbles or dark stones
Sand

ORIGIN:

In Togo, where this game originated, *ataklui* means "small black marble" or stone. Sometimes bigger marbles or small rocks are used, and these are called *bamboz*. This game is best played at the beach.

HOW TO PLAY:

1. A shallow trench (or channel) is dug with sand piled up on both sides. It's best to have the beginning of the trench at a high point, with a decline leading to a small, round pit. The trench can have curves in it and the length can vary.

2. With flicks of the thumb, each player (who starts off with ten marbles) shoots three marbles. The object is to have as many marbles as possible reach the pit. It's okay to smooth out or pat down the bottom and sides of the trench, but not too much, because part of the challenge is the texture of the sand.

3. Every time a marble reaches the pit, that player takes it back; the other ones remain stuck in the trench. The players take turns, each one dropping out when she has no more marbles. The player with marbles remaining after an equal number of turns is the winner.

4. The outcome of the game can be made more difficult: The last player with marbles flicks them through the channel. She then wins only if at least half of the remaining marbles reach the pit.

BANYOKA

Number of Players: 12 to 30
Age: 6 to 10
Equipment: Natural objects (especially thick grass)

ORIGIN:

Though associated with Zambia, the game was played by the Bemba tribe who lived in what is now both Zambia and the southern part of Zaire. *Banyoka* means "the snakes," and apparently the game developed from observing these creatures roaming the region.

HOW TO PLAY:

1. Choose a play area that is a bit of an obstacle course, with bushes and large rocks. For younger players, it's probably best to have the starting point be atop a small hill. You can create an obstacle course using toys, pillows, boxes, and cartons.

2. The players divide into two groups, each group having at least six.

3. Each group becomes a Snake by the players sitting one behind the other on the ground, legs spread and hands placed on the shoulders of the player in front, or arms wrapped around his chest.

4. Each Snake moves forward by the players swaying their bodies back and forth. The Snakes can sing a song.

5. The object for each Snake is to reach a designated finish line first. But the real fun of the game is to maneuver around bushes, rocks, and/or other objects, to "slither" around and over them while remaining connected to each other.

6. The game can also be played with one Snake. The competitive aspect is gone, replaced by a follow-the-leader quality. The "head" of the Snake decides the direction, turning one way then another and choosing which obstacles to go across or around. If the line is long enough, it's fun for players to deal with a new obstacle or change of direction while players farther behind are still coping with the previous one.

BATHING GAME

Number of Players: 10 to 20
Age: 8 to 12
Equipment: None

ORIGIN:

This game is attributed to Guinea. However, though it's an easy game to play, it can't be played in all African countries — or many states in the United States. Why? Because it was played on the beach. Loose, sandy soil can be substituted.

HOW TO PLAY:

1. Each player builds a mound of sand and sits on top of it. The players should face the same direction. If there's enough space available, the mounds can be in a circle about two feet apart.

2. At a signal, each player raises herself on her arms and swings her feet forward, attempting to land atop the next sand mound.

3. A player is "out" if his feet touch the sand between mounds. The game continues until one player is left.

BEWARE THE ANTELOPE

Number of Players: 10 to 20
Age: 6 to 8
Equipment: None

ORIGIN:

In the Congo, the antelope was considered a prize catch for hunters and a challenge because of its swiftness. This game, played by the children of the Luba Kasai tribe, turns the hunt around.

HOW TO PLAY:

1. Boundaries should be fixed, either natural ones or lines drawn on the ground.

2. A player is chosen to be an Antelope, who stands in the middle of the playing area, with the other children surrounding him a few feet away.

3. Guess what? The Hunters don't chase Antelope, he chases them! Every player he tags or who runs past a boundary also becomes an Antelope. The game continues until no hunters are left. The last player tagged becomes the Antelope in a new game.

BIASSON

Number of Players: 6 to 12
Age: 8 to 12
Equipment: String
Thin rope with a loop tied at one end
Corncob
Leaves

ORIGIN:

This creative skill game is attributed to the Ivory Coast. Corn has long been an important part of meals, and during harvests there are many ears available for children's play.

HOW TO PLAY:

1. Use the string to tie a bunch of leaves securely to one end of the corncob.

2. Players divide into two teams. Each team stands about six feet (or more) behind a line drawn in the ground.

TIE LEAVES WITH STRING

3. A player tosses the corncob into the air and toward the other team. A player on the other team, holding the rope, tries to catch the corncob within the loop before it hits the ground. If he's unsuccessful, the other team gets to toss again.

4. When the corncob is caught (the tied bunch of leaves makes this easier), the player removes it from the loop. The instant he does, the players on the other team can begin to run away. The first player, allowed to run as close as the dividing line, throws the corncob. If it touches an opposing player, the first player's team scores a point, and the other team must toss the corncob again.

5. If a player isn't touched by the thrown corncob, it's the other team's turn to toss it. The game continues, alternating in this way (and, on each team, the players doing the tossing and catching), until one team scores 10 points.

BIG SNAKE

Number of Players: 15 to 20
Age: 8 to 12
Equipment: None

ORIGIN:

This game, good for exercise, teamwork, and decision-making, is from Ghana.

HOW TO PLAY:

1. One player is designated as the Snake. A box about 10 feet square is drawn in the sand to be his home. It's also a good idea to set boundaries beyond which the other players cannot go.

2. The other players start running. When the Snake tags a player, she joins hands with him, becoming part of the snake, and together they go after other players. As more are tagged, Snake becomes longer. Any player part of Snake can tag a runner.

3. The "pieces" of the Snake must remain together. If they separate, they must return home where Snake is re-formed, and the chase begins again. The object of the game is to tag all the players so that they form one big Snake.

4. One strategy tip: When Snake gets big enough, it might be able to surround the remaining players and thus more easily catch them.

BIVOE EBUMA

("Clap Ball")

Number of Players: 10 to 20
Age: 8 to 12
Equipment: A ball (or even a round fruit!)

ORIGIN:

This game was usually played in the middle of a village street in Angola.

HOW TO PLAY:

1. In the dirt or sand, draw a line long enough that the number of youngsters playing can stand on either side in equal rows facing each other. Each row should be about 6 feet away from the line.

2. A player is selected to make the first toss. The ball can be thrown to any player on the other side of the line.

3. The ball is kept in play by tossing it from one row to the other. Each time it is caught, the other players clap and stamp their feet once.

4. Any player in the row can catch the ball, but no one may step over the line. If the ball is dropped (don't worry, you're not out), the one who tossed it gets to throw again.

5. The game is most exciting if the players try to decrease the time between tosses — and the rhythm of clapping and stomping becomes faster.

BLINDFOLD HORSE RACE

Number of Players: 12 to 20
Age: 8 to 12
Equipment: Any kind of cloth that can serve as a blindfold
Cans, boxes, miscellaneous objects

ORIGIN:

This game, which is especially fun for players who enjoy pretending, is associated with Nigeria.

HOW TO PLAY:

1. An "obstacle course" is laid out by using cans, boxes, or other small objects.

2. The players divide into pairs, and one member of each pair is chosen as the Horse. He should be able to support his partner, who as Rider is carried on his back. The Horse wears the blindfold.

3. The pairs navigate the obstacle course. The Rider guides the Horse without talking — pulling gently on the Horse's ears or tapping shoulders to signal direction and speed changes.

4. Players who bump into an obstacle must stop and "whinny" loudly before continuing.

5. There are two ways to determine winners: (a) The pairs can all start off at once and the Horse and Rider who reach the end of the course first are the winners; or (b) The pairs go one after another with a "timekeeper" keeping track of how long it takes each team to finish, with the shortest time resulting in a winner.

BOKWELE

Number of Players: 15 to 20
Age: 8 to 12
Equipment: Beans, small stones, or marbles

ORIGIN:

There are really two somewhat different games called Bokwele, both of which originated in the Congo (now Zaire).

HOW TO PLAY GAME #1:

1. Players are divided into two teams, though there can be three teams if that's more manageable.

2. Each team draws a circle on the ground. Within the circles each team places its objects. It's a good idea for each team to either have different objects, or have the same but different-colored objects.

3. At a signal, the players run around crying "Bokwele," as they try to steal the other team's (or teams') objects without being tagged. Tagged team members must stand aside.

4. The team that collects all the other team's objects is the winner.

HOW TO PLAY GAME #2:

1. In this version, it's best if there are no more than two teams. Also, in place of small objects, two long poles, about twice as tall as the players, are required.

2. Each team has a pole marked with light- and dark-colored rings. If a tree branch is used, you can peel off rings of bark.

3. At a signal, one player from each team climbs the pole, with teammates holding it upright. Not only must the player hold the light-ringed circles, but during the climb she must say "Bokwele" over and over without taking a breath.

4. The player who reaches the top first or is still climbing and calling when the other player runs out of breath scores a point.

5. Players from each team then take a turn. This continues until every player has had a turn. The team with the most points wins.

BOOKO

("Onide Comes")

Number of Players: 8 to 20
Age: 6 to 10
Equipment: A stone

ORIGIN:

This game comes from Nigeria, and more specifically from the Yoruba tribe.

HOW TO PLAY:

1. A player chosen as leader holds the stone in her hand. Another player runs off to hide.

2. The remaining children sit on the ground and hold out their hands. The leader passes among them, touching hands with the stone. The players can chant:

> Onide comes,
> Saworo, Onide comes.
> All right, Onide,
> Come and inspect us.

3. The leader places the stone secretly in one player's hand. She calls "Onide!" and the player who has hidden returns.

4. The players keep their arms out. Onide has three guesses to determine which player is holding the stone. If he's successful, he sits among the players and the one who held the stone becomes Onide. If unsuccessful, he goes and hides again.

5. This is not necessarily a competitive game, but if they want to (and the group is small enough) the players can keep track of who guessed successfully most often.

CAT AND LYNX

Number of Players: 10 to 20
Age: 6 to 10
Equipment: Cartons or boxes

ORIGIN:

This game is associated with the Bushmen of South Africa, most of whom live in and around the Kalahari Desert. In addition to having fun, it was a way for youngsters to learn the characteristics of certain animals, knowledge that would help them later when hunting. The lynx, though not the fastest mammal in Africa (that honor goes to the cheetah, which can run up to fifty-five miles an hour), is the fastest one the Bushmen encountered.

HOW TO PLAY:

1. The players divide into two teams, choosing which team will be Lynx and which Cat. Each team stands in a line, and the lines are about 25 feet apart.

2. Scattered in the space between the teams are up to a dozen boxes, but if there are natural obstacles, like small bushes or large rocks, those are fine too.

3. A member of each team walks to the center of the open area. They then gently "insult" each other. For example, Lynx might say, "I'm hungry, and I think I'll eat you." Cat replies, "You think so, but you are too slow and lazy." "I'm fast enough, and smarter too," Lynx boasts. Cat responds, "You'll go hungry today because you can't catch me."

4. Any form of dialogue can by used, but "Catch me" is the key phrase. As soon as it is uttered, the chase is on, with Lynx trying to catch Cat. They run in and around and among the obstacles. They can't jump over them, and Lynx can't reach over an obstacle to tag Cat.

5. Meanwhile, the other players are clapping and counting. When they reach twenty and the Cat hasn't been caught, the two players return to their teams and two different players repeat the scene. However, if Cat is caught, he joins the Lynx team.

6. There are two ways to win the game. First, if all the Cats are caught, the Lynx team wins. But if every Lynx has had a turn and more than half the Cats remain, the Cat team is the winner.

CATCH YOUR TAIL

Number of Players: 12 to 20
Age: 6 to 10
Equipment: Handkerchiefs or strips of cloth

ORIGIN:

This game, which is fun exercise, is attributed to Nigeria.

HOW TO PLAY:

1. Divide the players into two equal teams.

2. The players stand in two rows, and the players on each team grasp each other around the waist. The player at the end has a handkerchief, or "tail," tucked into his belt or pants waist at the back. The player at the other end is designated as the captain.

3. At a signal, the teams start moving so that the captains can try to snatch the tail of the other team. Players must remain connected to each other. Part of the fun is a team trying to give chase while eluding pursuit at the same time.

4. If there are enough players and they think it will be fun, three teams can compete.

5. You can play ten times, and the team that has captured the most tails wins.

CATCHING A LENDU

Number of Players: 6 to 10
Age: 6 to 8
Equipment: Leaves
Thin branches or reeds
Sheet or old net

ORIGIN:

Pygmy children of the Congo counted this game among their favorites because it imitated the hunting of adults. Almost any animal can be used, but a popular one was the lendu, a small antelope with two sharp horns.

HOW TO PLAY:

1. One player is selected to be the Lendu, and two players choose a spot to stand holding the sheet.

2. The other players hold the leaves and branches. When the Lendu enters the "clearing" (with two extended fingers to simulate horns), the players shake the leaves and branches at it but don't touch the Lendu. In fact, the Lendu is supposed to avoid being touched.

3. The object is to maneuver the Lendu toward the sheet or net where it is caught. The Lendu tries to remain free for a designated period of time – say, 30 seconds. If it is successful, it can choose to go again or play one of the other roles.

CHIGORO DANDA

Number of Players: 3 to 10
Age: 8 to 12
Equipment: Three poles or long tree branches

ORIGIN:

This game is attributed to Zimbabwe, but it's thought it may have come originally from India because in one of that country's languages *danda* means "pole" or "long stick" and there is a game there called Guli Danda. However, the rhythmic tapping and clapping of Chigoro Danda is African.

HOW TO PLAY:

1. The players alternate so that three play each game.

2. Place two of the poles (4 to 5 feet long) on the ground parallel to each other, 4 feet apart. The third pole is laid across the middle of the parallel poles. Two players sit at each end of the cross bar, and the third is in the middle, straddling the cross pole.

3. The two seated players lift the cross pole up and down, tapping the parallel poles. The surrounding players clap, and a rhythm is established. Start off very slowly.

4. The third player hops onto the cross pole every time it is placed down, then hops off.

5. The raising and lowering of the cross pole and the clapping and hopping increase in speed. The game ends when the third player fails to hop on the cross pole.

6. The players rotate so everyone has a turn hopping and manipulating the cross pole. Someone can time how long the third player stays in each game, but it's probably more useful to have each player keep count.

(An adult supervisor can help make sure the game doesn't become fast-paced enough to cause an injury.)

CROCODILE RIDES

Number of Players: 6 to 12
Age: 6 to 10
Equipment: None

ORIGIN:

This game was played by the Paga tribe, which lived in the northern section of Ghana. A similar game called "Alligator Crawl" is played by youngsters who live in swamp areas of Georgia and Florida.

HOW TO PLAY:

1. Players divide into pairs, and each pair decides which one will be the Crocodile and which the Rider.

2. A large circle is drawn or marked on the ground that represents a pond, home to the crocodiles. About twenty feet away a line is drawn representing the starting point, where the players stand.

3. At a signal each Crocodile begins to crawl toward home using elbows and bellies. Riders walk alongside to guide the Crocodiles, and to challenge any other Crocodile who isn't crawling the right way.

4. The first pair to reach the pond is the winner.

DA GA

Number of Players: 12 to 20
Age: 8 to 12
Equipment: None

ORIGIN:

This game is from Ghana, and *da ga* means "boa constrictor," a snake. In the United States, boa constrictors are found — rarely! — only as pets.

HOW TO PLAY:

1. Create an area on the ground about 10 feet square as the "Home of the Snake."

2. A player is chosen to stand inside the area, and the others surround the area.

3. The first player reaches out to touch any one of the other youngsters. The two hold hands and then reach out (using only the free hand) to touch other players. Each youngster touched joins the Snake by holding hands, and the Snake grows in length.

4. The surrounding youngsters can sing or dance or otherwise move about to avoid being tagged but must stay close to the area's perimeter. As more players are touched, they become part of the growing Snake.

5. The last player remaining begins to form a new Snake in the next game.

FEATHER GAME

Number of Players: 4 to 10
Age: 8 to 12
Equipment: A lot of quill feathers
A nearby tree

ORIGIN:

This activity originated in South Africa. However, it's easy to see that youngsters in any African country could have played this game.

HOW TO PLAY:

1. Mark off a distance, say six feet, from a tree. The trunk's width can depend on how challenging players want to make the game.

2. To begin, one player should refrain from participating to serve as the leader.

3. Each participating youngster has a feather. At a signal from the leader, they toss the feathers at the tree.

4. The player whose feather has struck the tree or who has come the closest becomes the leader. If more than one player has hit the mark, there can be a playoff.

5. Have double the number of rounds as there are players, plus one. For example, if there are six players, have thirteen rounds.

6. The player who has become leader the most is the winner. If there is a tie, have three playoff rounds.

THE FISHERMEN

Number of Players: 15 to 20
Age: 6 to 10
Equipment: A long rope

ORIGIN:

This game was played by children in Ghana who wanted to imitate a grownup food-gathering practice.

HOW TO PLAY:

1. By drawing a line or lines, a "fishing area" is created — it can be a large circle, square or rectangle. Beyond the boundaries is the "safe area."

2. Four players are selected to be the fishermen, and they stand within the fishing area holding the rope and pretending that it's a net.

3. The game begins with the other players cavorting within the fishing area as they pretend to be swimming fish. The fishermen sing an appropriate short song or a verse. When they stop singing, they use the "net" to surround as many fish as possible. Fish can swim to freedom by running to the safe area. Those who have been caught are out.

4. The caught fish become fishermen, joining the others with the net. The fish return and the routine is repeated.

5. The object is to catch all the fish. The last four caught become the fishermen in a new game.

GAZELLE STALKING

Number of Players: 6 to 10
Age: 8 to 12
Equipment: Handkerchiefs or strips of cloth
Cans filled with pebbles

ORIGIN:

This game is not attributed to one specific country but to the area in and around the Kalahari Desert, and to the Zulu and Bantu tribes who spoke "click" languages, so called because of clicking sounds made with the tongue on the roof of the mouth. The game developed from the practice of hunting springbok – South African gazelle. Versions of this game were played in England and Scotland as Deer Stalking, and by American Indians as Buffalo Hunt.

HOW TO PLAY:

1. Two players are chosen to be Gazelle and Stalker. Both are blindfolded by handkerchiefs. They are taken by the others to opposite sides of a field.

2. The object is for Stalker to find and tag Gazelle. Obviously, as they move about the field, Gazelle must be as quiet as possible. But there's a catch: The other players, the Watchers, have spread out in the field, each one holding a can. When Gazelle comes near a player, he shakes the can three times, the rattling or "clicking" pebbles sending a signal to Stalker.

3. It's best to set a time limit, say ten minutes or less. Whoever is successful, Stalker or Gazelle (by going uncaught until time is up), is allowed to choose his next role – Stalker, Gazelle, or Watcher.

GRAB IT

Number of Players: 8 to 10
Age: 8 to 12
Equipment: Handkerchief or piece of cloth

ORIGIN:

This exercise and thinking game is from Ghana, yet there is a similar game familiar to children in the United States called Steal the Bacon.

HOW TO PLAY:

1. Standing about six feet apart are the players, divided into two equal teams. Placed halfway between the teams on the ground is the handkerchief.

2. At a signal, two players from each team run forward. Their goal is for one of them to grab the handkerchief and return to his team without being tagged by his two opponents.

3. The successful team scores a point. However, if a player tags the person who grabbed the handkerchief, his team scores a point. Two different players for each team take the next turn.

4. The first team to score ten points wins.

Note: It might be a good idea to determine how physical the game can be. For example, one player may or may not be allowed to "block" for his teammate, who is trying to escape with the handkerchief.

HAWK AND HENS

Number of Players: 15 to 20
Age: 6 to 8
Equipment: None

ORIGIN:

This game was played by the Baratosi tribe in the southern section of Rhodesia, now called Zimbabwe.

HOW TO PLAY:

1. A player is selected to be Hawk, and the others are the Hens.

2. The players can designate certain spots as "safety zones." These can be natural objects, like trees, bushes, or small hills, or with a stick or chalk circles can be drawn on the ground. Keep in mind that the fewer safety zones, the greater challenge.

3. After the players have spread out among the safety zones, the Hawk gives a cry. That's the signal for the players to run to different safety zones.

4. As birds of prey do, this Hawk tries to tag the running Hens as they "fly" to safety. The tagged Hens stay to one side.

5. The last Hen caught is offered a choice: He/she can become the Hawk, or can designate another player to be the bird of prey.

INZEMA

Number of Players: 8 to 1
Age: 8 to 10
Equipment: A ball about the size of a soccer ball
Sticks or thin branches

ORIGIN:

This game was played by children in Uganda who wanted to practice for the day when they would be allowed to go hunting.

HOW TO PLAY:

1. A player is selected as the bowler, and she holds the ball. The others form two lines about 10 feet apart.

2. The ball is rolled swiftly between the two lines and the players toss their "spears" at it.

3. The first player to strike the ball becomes the bowler, and the former bowler goes to stand at the end of that player's line.

JUMPING THE BEANBAG

Number of Players: 6 to 10
Age: 6 to 8
Equipment: Rope
Beanbag

ORIGIN:

When this game was played by children in Nigeria, players often made their own beanbag by taping beans or pebbles in a piece of thin cloth. You can do this too.

HOW TO PLAY:

1. Tie one end of the rope securely around the beanbag.

2. One player is selected to hold the rope, and the other players form a circle around her.

3. The center player swings the extended rope as low to the ground as possible. Those in the circle jump over the beanbag. If a foot touches the beanbag, that player is out.

4. The last player left gets to swing the beanbag in the next game.

KAMESHI NE MPUKU
("The Cat and the Rat")

Number of Players: Up to 30
Age: 8 to 12
Equipment: None

ORIGIN:

This particular version has been attributed to the Luba tribe in the Congo, but many tribes played various forms of this popular game.

HOW TO PLAY:

1. The players stand in four equal rows, creating three aisles among them. In each row the players hold hands. One player is chosen to be the caller.

2. A player is chosen to be the Rat, and another is chosen to be the Cat. At a signal, Rat runs up and down the aisles with Cat in pursuit.

3. The caller shouts, "*Mpuki ekale,*" which means "Let the Rat stop." The players in the rows drop hands and join hands with the row across. This changes the direction of the aisles and Rat must adapt to the change or be trapped by a barrier of joined hands.

4. At regular intervals the caller shouts and the aisles change directions. When Rat is caught, two new players become Cat and Rat, though being successful Cat can choose to remain or to become Rat.

5. A time limit can be set. For example, if one minute passes (a player could be designated as the timekeeper) and Rat has eluded capture, he or she wins and can choose who does what.

KHOLO EVEAWO

("The Two Friends")

Number of Players: 9 to 19
Age: 6 to 10
Equipment: None

ORIGIN:

Though there is some information that this game was played in Togo, it is mostly associated with Ghana.

HOW TO PLAY:

1. The players line up in pairs, with the one person chosen as It standing at the head of the double rows.

2. It announces, *"Mele Kholo dim,"* or "I am looking for a friend," and claps hands. The pair at the end of the rows run forward on either side. As soon as they're past It, It runs after them, trying to catch one before the pair meets up again.

3. If the pair meets, they stand at the front of the rows and It tries again. If It catches one, they become the pair who stands at the front, with the remaining player becoming It.

4. The game continues until each pair has had a chance to run.

KINI O NI IYE?

("Who Has Feathers?")

Number of Players: Up to 20
Age: 8 to 12
Equipment: Long or wide leaves

ORIGIN:

This game is associated with Nigeria, but it was probably played almost anywhere in Africa except desert regions.

HOW TO PLAY:

1. The players sit on the ground. Each one holds a leaf. One player, selected to be the leader, can remain standing.

2. The leader asks, "Does a bird have feathers?" The players should reply, "*Beni*," or "Yes." The next question is, "Does a house have feathers?" The response should be, "*Beko*," or "No."

3. The leader keeps asking questions that require a yes or no answer. The player who answers incorrectly loses his or her leaf.

4. The winner is the player who retains a leaf the longest, and he or she becomes the leader.

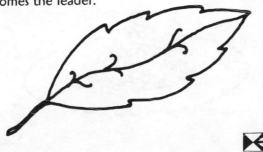

KUWAKHA NCHUWA

Number of Players: 4 to 10

Age: 6 to 8

Equipment: Stones (as many as 100!)
A pebble

ORIGIN:

This game, most often played by girls, came from Malawi.

HOW TO PLAY:

1. A circle is drawn on the ground, and in the center, in one big pile, the stones are placed. Players sit just outside the circle.

2. The player selected to hold the pebble tosses it into the air. He grabs a stone and then attempts to catch the descending pebble with the same hand holding the stone. If he is unsuccessful, the stone is returned. If he is successful, the stone is set aside.

3. Each player tosses the pebble ten times and keeps his own pile of collected stones. When everyone has had a turn, the player with the most stones wins.

LOOP THE SHUTTLECOCK

This game is almost identical to Biasson, described earlier. However, in addition to the Ivory Coast, Loop the Shuttlecock has origins in Ghana as well.

MOONSHINE BABY

Number of Players: 6 to 8
Age: 6 to 10
Equipment: Stones, small sticks, or chalk

ORIGIN:

This game comes from Ghana. It was also played on a beach using shells.

HOW TO PLAY:

1. One player is chosen as "It." He goes far enough away that he can't observe the other players. (No peeking!)

2. The remaining players choose one to be the Baby. He lies on the ground, and his companions outline him, using stones, sticks, or chalk. When the outline is completed, he gets up and joins the others. (Try to make the outline as detailed as possible, perhaps indicating differences in type of hair or clothing.)

3. It is called back. It then must guess whose outline is on the ground. (Depending on the age or number of players, It can be allowed up to three guesses.)

4. If It guesses incorrectly, off he goes again, and a new outline is made. If he guesses right, another player is chosen to be It.

MOTO

("Fire")

Number of Players: 18 to 22
Age: 6 to 8
Equipment: None

ORIGIN:

This game, which involves the fun of pretending, is from Tanganyika.

HOW TO PLAY:

1. With the exception of one person selected as Leader, the players form two circles, one inside the other.

2. Players in the inner circle are the Children, who squat or kneel, and the players on the outer circle are the Parents, who place their hands on the Child in front of them.

3. The leader calls, "*Moto!*" At this, the Parents run around the inner circle calling, "*Kilimani,*" which means, "On the mountain-top!" This goes on for as long as the leader calls, "*Moto!*"

4. When the leader shouts, "*Moto kabisa,*" or "Extremely hot fire," he runs to stand behind a Child. All the Parents stand still behind a Child. The one left "childless" becomes the next leader.

5. To add to the drama, the Children can pretend to be afraid of the fire.

MPUKU MU KINA KYANDJI ("The Rat in His Hole")

Number of Players: Up to 30
Age: 8 to 12
Equipment: None

ORIGIN:

There are several variations of the game using other animals, but this particular one is attributed to the Chokwe tribe in the southern section of the Congo and Angola. It is a variation of the game on page 47.

HOW TO PLAY:

1. One player is chosen to be the Rat, and another to be the Cat.

2. The rest of the players form a circle, feet and elbows touching, facing Rat in the center of the circle, which is his hole. The Cat roams outside the circle.

3. At a point of his choosing, Cat tries to enter the circle by squeezing between two players, who try to resist the effort. If Cat succeeds, Rat runs out of his hole (players in the circle allow him free passage) and the Cat gives chase by exiting the same way. If Rat gets back around to the same entrance, he enters his hole and the players close ranks.

4. Rat can choose to leave his hole, thinking Cat isn't looking. Also, Cat can pretend to be distracted, then chase Rat once he leaves his hole. The more daring the Rat, the more fun the game!

5. When Cat catches Rat, he becomes Rat and a new Cat is chosen from among the other players.

NTE-TOO
("Playing with Seeds")

Number of Players: 2 to 4
Age: 6 to 10
Equipment: Acorns or similar nuts

ORIGIN:

In Ghana "seeds" could mean anything small and round that came from a tree. In the United States, acorns are probably best.

HOW TO PLAY:

1. Two kneeling players face each other across two feet of bare ground. In front of each one is a row of ten or twelve nuts.

2. By either pushing or flicking it with his thumb, one player rolls a nut toward his opponent's line. If it touches one of his opponent's nuts, that nut is "captured" and set aside. The rolled nut is retrieved and rolled again. If it hits nothing, it belongs to the opponent, who then rolls one of his own nuts.

3. The object is to set aside more nuts than one's opponent. Teams of two can also play.

4. Depending on the age of the players, there can be an added challenge that involves greater skill (aside from making the rows of nuts farther apart). Each player can mark a line in the ground a foot behind the row of nuts. Then, if a player misses and his acorn goes past the back line, the other player not only captures that acorn but is given a bonus one.

STONE GAME

Number of Players: 6 to 8
Age: 8 to 12
Equipment: Pebbles or small stones or acorns

ORIGIN:

This game comes from the northern section of Zimbabwe.

HOW TO PLAY:

1. Dig a small hole and drop into it the stones. The players sit in a circle around the hole.

2. To begin the game, a player plucks one stone and tosses it high. While it is in the air, that player grabs more stones from the hole yet must be prepared to catch the tossed one when it returns.

3. If he catches it, he puts it aside, returns the collected stones to the hole, takes one and tosses it again. The game is repeated until he doesn't catch the falling stone.

4. All the players take a turn. When everyone has gone, the player with the most stones set aside is the winner. If there's a tie, the players can participate in a playoff.

TSETSETSE

Number of Players: 3
Age: 6 to 10
Equipment: Stones
              Chalk

ORIGIN:

When you see how this game is played, you'll probably exclaim, "This is Hopscotch!" Yes, essentially it is. And it's possible that the American version came from elsewhere. But this particular game is from South Africa.

HOW TO PLAY:

1. The players decide who will go first, second, and third.

2. Draw a ground plan in sand or soil, or on a hard surface with chalk. The plan includes four connected rectangles in a row, three feet long by six feet wide, and an oval area at the near end.

3. The first player stands in the oval area. She places a stone in the first rectangle and hops into that space on one foot. By continuously hopping, she kicks the stone into the subsequent rectangles and hops into them. If she uses the other foot or kicks the stone out of the next space, she's out.

4. When the player has reached the fourth rectangle, she calls, "*Ara-uru!*" She can then pick up the stone and hop backward to the oval space, where she lands on two feet and calls, "Out game!"

5. Okay, here's a supertricky part: The first player to successfully complete the round gets to stand in the oval with her back turned to the rectangles and toss the stone over her shoulder. If it lands in a space, she marks it with an X.

6. The other players cannot land on the X — if they do, they're out. The second and third players follow the same procedure.

7. The first player to mark an X in all four rectangles is the winner.

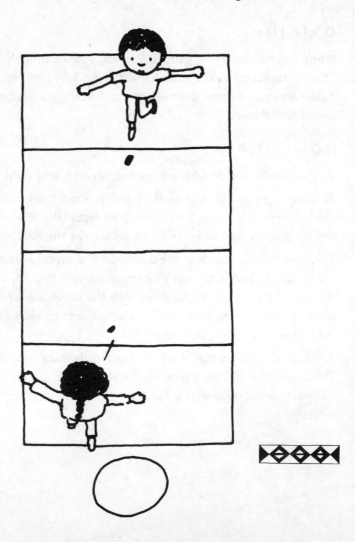

TUG OF WAR

Number of Players: 15 to 20
Age: 8 to 12
Equipment: A long rope

ORIGIN:

Various versions of Tug of War are played all over the world. This particular version is attributed to the Banyankole tribe of Uganda. It was a standard practice to arrange marriages between families, and it was the custom to pretend that one side or the other, groom's or bride's family, did not want the marriage ceremony to take place. (Traditionally, it was almost always the bride's family, and they always wound up giving in!)

HOW TO PLAY:

1. Divide the players into two teams, and each player chooses a leader, who stands at the head of the line. Also, one player stands off to the side — in the traditional game, this person would be the Bride.

2. Draw a dividing line in the ground. Teams stand on either side, holding onto the rope.

3. At a signal, the tugging begins. In the traditional game (where the Groom's team was allowed to win!), the successful team is the one that tugs the other team over the line, and that team is awarded the bride. However, in this game, the player standing to the side should be awarded to the losing team, which is given another chance to win.

4. If that team is again unsuccessful, it's probably a good idea to rearrange the teams!

TWO FRIENDS

Number of Players: 12 to 20
Age: 8 to 12
Equipment: None

ORIGIN:

This running game is associated with Ghana, but is also known to have been played in neighboring Togo. (Note that this game is quite similar to a couple of other games in this section.) This game, with a few variations, is also played in Sweden as Widower's Game and in the United States as Last Couple Out, indicating how universal some African games are.

HOW TO PLAY:

1. One player is selected as It and stands in front of the other players who have lined up in pairs, holding hands.

2. Raising clasped hands, It calls, "I'm looking for a friend." The last couple starts to run forward on either side of the line and pass It.

3. It gives chase and tries to tag one of the running players before they join hands. If she succeeds, the other player becomes her friend and the tagged player becomes It. Otherwise, It stays It until she finds a friend, or perhaps after three chances is offered a friend.

INDOOR GAMES

Indoor games were usually played by younger children who were being supervised by adults, or by older children who were inside because of bad weather. For some of the games in this section, you will need enough space in a room for the activity and, to be on the safe side, make sure nothing breakable is within reach. Mostly, though, these games are suitable for living rooms, basements, and small courtyards.

BEAN HOLE TOSS

Number of Players: 3
Age: 6 to 10
Equipment: Metal bowl
Brush and paper plate
30 beans

ORIGIN:

Children in the northern part of West Africa were known to play this game, for a very good reason — the climate in that region is good for growing legumes, so there were usually plenty of beans to spare for recreation. This game helps to increase tossing and counting skills, but mostly it's just plain fun.

HOW TO PLAY:

1. Place the metal bowl in the center of the room.

2. Select a spot in any direction from the bowl that is five feet away, though the distance can vary depending on the age of the players.

3. Divide the 30 beans in half, giving 15 each to two players. The third stands ready with the brush and plate.

4. The first player tosses her handful at the bowl. She picks up the beans that landed in the bowl. (Sorry — if they went in but bounced out, they don't count!) The beans around the bowl are left there.

5. The second player does the same. When he's done, the third player sweeps up the loose beans.

6. The winner is the player who gets all his/her beans in the bowl. However, given the bouncy nature of beans, it might be a good idea to set a limit, say three rounds, and the player with the fewest beans left in her hand is the winner.

7. The third player challenges the winner, and the game is repeated.

8. *Bonus:* If you use the rounds system, a way to determine the ultimate winner is for the two players after each game to jot down how many beans they have left. Then, after 6, 9, or 12 games (with three players, the number of games has to be divisible by three), add up the beans each player has left. The one with the lowest total is the champion.

COCK-A-LOO

Number of Players: 6 to 8
Age: 6 to 8
Equipment: None

ORIGIN:

This game was played in Ethiopia, usually when an older youngster was babysitting children who were getting a bit restless waiting for their parents to return. It is a "waiting" game in which one player gets to do his/her best rooster imitation.

HOW TO PLAY:

1. One player (an older child, if one is present, or a grownup) is chosen to be Mother. She sits on the floor or on a low stool.

2. Another child is selected to be It. He hides his head in Mother's lap so that he can't see. The other players hide nearby, behind chairs or doors.

3. While the players are hiding, It asks Mother, "Cock-a-loo?" She answers, "No, the sun is not up yet." This is repeated five times, with It sounding like he's crowing.

4. Mother says, "Now the sun is up." It stands and looks for the others. They, meanwhile, try to quietly return to Mother.

5. A player who touches Mother before being tagged by It gets to go hide again. Those who are tagged stand aside.

6. Once everyone has been tagged, or a prearranged time limit has expired, the next It is selected from among the tagged players.

FOX

Number of Players: 8 to 12
Age: 6 to 8
Equipment: Handkerchief

ORIGIN:

This game was played throughout the northern and eastern parts of Africa, yet is most often associated with Egypt.

HOW TO PLAY:

1. One player is chosen to be Fox and the others form a circle facing one another.

2. Holding the handkerchief, Fox slowly walks around the circle, talking and asking questions about anything on her mind to distract the others.

3. Fox drops the handkerchief behind a player. (The children in the circle shouldn't be peeking!) Fox runs twice around the circle. The players look for the handkerchief, and the one who had it dropped behind him picks it up and chases Fox.

4. If the player catches Fox, Fox must try again. If the player doesn't tag Fox, he becomes Fox.

5. Try to let every player take a turn being Fox.

HABA GABA

Number of Players: 2 to 6
Age: 6 to 12
Equipment: Several beanbags
Large piece of cardboard
Scissors

ORIGIN:

This game was developed in Sierra Leone, a mountainous region of West Africa. (It was also played in nearby Portuguese and Spanish Guinea and French Senegal.) Sierra Leone has a slightly unusual history. During the American Revolution, a number of black families supported and fought for the British. In gratitude (and perhaps to help them avoid retribution) the British brought these families to Africa and founded Sierra Leone. The descendants of these families came to call themselves Creoles and they eventually spoke Krio, a combination of English, French, Spanish, and Portuguese. The game they invented was named *haba*, a Spanish word for "bean," and *gaba*, which is short for *gabacha*, which means "Frenchy."

HOW TO PLAY:

1. Cut out three holes in the cardboard and number them 1, 2, and 3. The holes must be of different sizes – two, three, and four inches in diameter.

2. Slant the cardboard at a 45-degree angle. It can be propped against the arm of a chair.

3. The players take turns standing ten feet from the board. (This can vary, depending on the players' ages.)

4. Each player tosses the same number of beanbags, say five, and they keep track of the number of points scored during each turn. (Points are scored according to which hole the beanbag passes through.) After a predetermined number of rounds — anywhere from six to ten — each player adds up his/her score. The highest score wins.

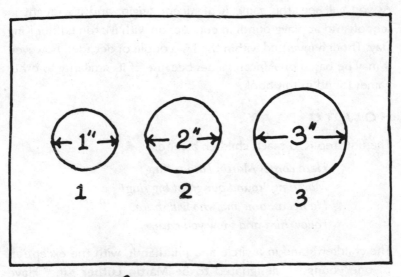

HERE COMES KING

Number of Players: 6 to 10
Age: Up to 8
Equipment: None

ORIGIN:

As you will see, this game is of recent origin, and it's taught in schools and at playgrounds in connection with Martin Luther King Day. Though invented within the last couple of decades, however, it may be based on African games because of its similarity to other games found in this book.

HOW TO PLAY:

The first step is to teach children a verse:

> *Here comes Martin Luther King*
> *Marching 'round our great big ring!*
> *He needs someone who will share.*
> *Follow him and show you care.*

The children stand in a circle and join hands, with the exception of one youngster designated to be Martin Luther King. Have "King" step around the circle while the children chant. At the word "care," King taps a child and runs around the circle to escape being tapped back. If King is able to take the place of the tapped child, then that youngster becomes King.

HOW MANY?

Number of Players: 4 to 8
Age: 8 to 12
Equipment: Beads, corn kernels, or pebbles

ORIGIN:

This guessing game was very popular in Tanganyika.

HOW TO PLAY:

1. African children often used roasted grain as "counters." In this case, you can use more readily available small objects. Each player holds between fifteen and twenty in one hand. (All players should have an equal number.)

2. A player puts from none to four counters into her other hand. She holds out her closed fist to another player and asks, "How many?"

3. If the other player guesses correctly, he gets all the counters. If he offers an incorrect guess, he must "pay" the other player the amount in her hand.

4. All the players take turns. The winner is the player who ends up with all the counters. A time limit can be set on the game, in which case when time is up the player with the most counters is the winner.

5. In Tanganyika, the first player to run out of counters was called *kiboko mjinga,* or "silly hippo."

KUDODA

Number of Players: 2 or more
Age: 6 to 8
Equipment: Marbles
Bowl

ORIGIN:

You'll quickly notice that this game is a familiar one. An original version, often played with stones or pebbles, can be found in Zimbabwe.

HOW TO PLAY:

1. Players sit in a circle.

2. Place the bowl (preferably a metal one) in the center. Fill it with about 20 marbles.

3. The first player takes a marble and tosses it into the air. (Not too high!) She then tries to pluck as many marbles as she can before catching the tossed marble.

4. Players in the circle take turns. When all the marbles have been collected, the person with the most is the winner.

LIBA

Number of Players: 2 or more
Age: 6 to 10
Equipment: Acorns or marbles

ORIGIN:

This game, which has two interesting twists, was played in East African countries.

HOW TO PLAY:

1. Place about two dozen acorns in a pile on the floor. Players sit in a circle around the pile.

2. The first player tosses an acorn in the air, then, before catching it, picks (one at a time) acorns from the pile.

3. One twist is that if the tossed acorn isn't caught, the acorns are returned to the pile.

4. Another twist is that if a player doesn't manage to pick at least three acorns, the acorns picked must be returned. Only three or more are "keepers."

5. The players take turns until the pile is gone. The player with the most acorns is the winner.

MATCHING FINGERS

Number of Players: 6
Age: 5 to 8
Equipment: Paper and pen/pencil

ORIGIN:

Northeast Africa. Though this game is associated with a certain region, it's easy to see that it could not only be common to the entire continent but was played elsewhere in the world, and may already be practiced in your neighborhood.

HOW TO PLAY:

1. Two pairs of partners play, each one sitting back-to-back. One of the nonplayers serves as a Watcher.

2. When the Watcher calls "Go!" all four players extend anywhere from one to four fingers. If both partners throw out the same number of fingers, 10 points are recorded on a pad for that team. (If none of the fingers match, try again.)

3. The team that didn't offer matching fingers is replaced by the third team and the process is repeated.

4. The team plays in round-robin fashion, and the first team to score 100 points wins.

MOTO MLIMANI

Number of Players: 5 to 10
Age: Up to 10
Equipment: None

ORIGIN:

This version is from Tanzania, although it's easy to see that it could have been played in almost any part of Africa.

HOW TO PLAY:

1. The players agree on a place, such as "mountain" or "river" or "forest."

2. After choosing a leader, who remains standing, they lie on their backs.

3. The leader shouts, "*Moto mlimani!*" which means "Fire on the mountain!" The players reply, "*Moto!*" The leader shouts, "*Moto mtoni!*" which means "Fire on the river!" The players respond, "*Moto!*" (You can also use English.)

4. When the leader shouts the designated place — mountain, river, village, forest, etc. — the players stand up. The player who stands last is out. (Also out is any player who stands before the designated place is named.)

5. The last player remaining becomes the new leader.

MY LITTLE BIRD

Number of Players: 8 to 12
Age: 6 to 10
Equipment: None

ORIGIN:

A version of this game, called Birds Fly, is played in the United States. The original version is associated with Tanganyika.

HOW TO PLAY:

1. The players stand together in a group, with the exception of one youngster who stands apart.

2. The player standing apart, in front of the group, calls out, "My little bird is lively," and flaps his arms. Then he quickly calls out the name of another bird or animal, such as, "Crow . . . flies!" or "Cow . . . flies!" and he flaps his arms again.

3. If what the player names really can fly, the group imitates his flapping arms. If it cannot fly, the players stand still.

4. Any player who flaps his/her arms in response to the naming of a nonflying animal is out. When all the players are out, the game begins again with a new caller.

5. To add to the fun: If only one player is left with the caller, a limit can be set on how many times the caller can try to trick her. For example, if after three tries the remaining player isn't out, she can be declared the winner and take over as caller.

NSUNSA

Number of Players: Up to 12
Age: 6 to 10
Equipment: None

ORIGIN:

This game is attributed to the Bamboma region of the Congo, yet it suggests that similar versions were played in many parts of Africa. There is evidence in history that this game was played between representatives of two villages as part of festivities.

HOW TO PLAY:

1. The players divide into two lines that face each other about five feet apart.

2. At a prearranged signal the child at the head of one line steps toward her counterpart and stops about two feet away.

3. All the other players clap three times.

4. At the third clap, the opponents grasp one another's forearms (but not in an aggressive manner).

5. (a) If they hold the same arm, say left to left, the challenger wins and the opponent goes to the end of the line, with everyone in the line moving up one place. (b) If they hold opposite arms, the challenger loses and goes to the end of her line.

6. After a certain amount of time, five or ten minutes, tally up the number of wins for each team. The team with the highest total is the champ.

NUMBERS

Number of Players: 10 to 15
Age: 6 and Under
Equipment: None

ORIGIN:

This game is attributed to the Ovimbundu tribe who live in what is now Zaire. Though a fun activity, it was used to help young children learn counting and the significance of numbers.

HOW TO PLAY:

Among a group of youngsters a leader is chosen, or an adult can be the caller. The children march in a circle around the room. When the leader calls out a number, say "four," the players divide into groups of four. (It's okay to have a group of less than four but not more than four.) They march again until the leader calls out a different number. There is no winner, but youngsters enjoy seeing how quickly they can divide into the called number.

To learn an African language and for an extra challenge, call out the numbers in the Ovimbundu language: *talu* (five), *qualla* (four), *tatu* (three), *vali* (two), and *mosi* (one).

PEBBLE COUNTING

Number of Players: 10 to 12
Age: 8 to 12
Equipment: Marbles or pebbles

ORIGIN:

Games very similar to this were played throughout Africa, but this one was a favorite in Ghana.

HOW TO PLAY:

1. On the floor is placed a long line of twenty or thirty marbles or pebbles. Players sit on either side.

2. A player at one end of the line stands, takes a deep breath, and walks along the line, crooning or singing a popular song. As he goes, he bends down to touch each marble or pebble.

3. If he gets to the end of the line without running out of breath, he picks up one marble or pebble.

4. Each player takes a turn. The game continues until every marble or pebble is picked up. The player who has collected the most is the winner.

PIE KALAH

Number of Players: 6 to 12
Age: Up to 10
Equipment: A small stone or ball

ORIGIN:

This simple game is claimed by several African countries, but it is most often associated with Liberia. Some people are unaware that the origin of Liberia was unusual: In the nineteenth century, a group of escaped slaves and freed black Americans chose to sail to Africa, where they founded their own country. Many of their descendants live there to this day.

HOW TO PLAY:

1. Two teams with an equal number of players are formed, and they stand only a few feet apart, facing each other. A leader for each team is chosen.

2. The leader picks up the stone, then secretly places it in the hand of a teammate.

3. The teams move close together. The team with the stone chants:

> *Ah! Pie ma yan ma kalah*
> *Ah! sa ma kalah gbon whala*
> *Yah! hail, yoah! gay lay, gay la.*

4. The team holds out their arms with hands closed. The leader of the other team calls, *"To kalah!"* ("Hand me the stone!") He tries to guess which hand holds the stone.

5. If he guesses correctly, the stone is given to his team. If he's wrong, the first team goes again.

6. After ten minutes, the team with the most correct guesses wins.

POISON

Number of Players: 8 to 12

Age: 10 and Under

Equipment: Handkerchief/cloth tied in a knot

ORIGIN:

This game comes from South Africa. And it's not as lethal as it sounds!

HOW TO PLAY:

1. One child is chosen to be It. The others form a circle around that player.

2. The tied handkerchief or cloth, the "poison," is placed in the center of the circle near It's feet.

3. It chooses a player whose task it is to take the poison — by hand, not mouth! — and that player is the Thief. The Thief joins It in the circle.

4. The circle of children shouts "Go!" and the players within the circle vie to take the poison and return to the empty spot in the circle.

5. Whoever doesn't get the poison and return to the circle is It. If the same youngster is unsuccessful after three tries, a new It is selected.

SHEEP AND HYENA

Number of Players: 10 to 12
Age: 6 to 8
Equipment: None

ORIGIN:

This game is similar to Cat and Rat, played in the United States. The version described here comes from Sudan.

HOW TO PLAY:

1. One player is chosen to be Sheep, and another is Hyena.

2. The remaining players form a circle. Hyena is on the outside, Sheep in the middle.

3. The circle moves slowly around to prevent Hyena from finding an opening to get to Sheep. But when Hyena does get through, he becomes Sheep and a different player is chosen as Hyena.

BOARD GAMES

Several cultures around the world claim to have produced the oldest board games, but Africa could have the strongest claim.

Evidence suggests that *mankala*, which in various forms may be the world's most popular board game, was played well over four thousand years ago. For example, wall paintings on the tomb of Rashepes, who ruled Egypt around 2500 B.C., show figures playing a game resembling mankala. Other existing records indicate that in subsequent centuries board games, including a form of checkers, were part of everyday life in Africa. Some findings by archaeologists suggest that board games existed as long as five thousand years ago in Africa, though it's possible they weren't games but record-keeping systems. Other evidence of board games dating from hundreds and even thousands of years ago has been found in what are now Zimbabwe, Uganda, Ethiopia, Ghana, and Zaire. In some cases, they were even used as part of religious ceremonies.

Many of the records indicate that the games were typically part of court life, meaning they were played by kings and queens and other levels of royalty. However, other findings show that in villages throughout Africa adults and children created their own rudimentary games of strategy, sometimes on boards and sometimes by moving objects across a diagram drawn in the ground. (Board games could be elaborate; for example, the Ashanti kings in Ghana had boards made of gold!) Such games were played for fun, of course, but other purposes included using board games as teaching tools and as part of religious observances. (More information about these games, some of them offered here, is available in *African Games of Strategy*, compiled by Louise Crane and published as part of the African Outreach Series by the University of Illinois.)

We've given board games their own section for two reasons: (1) While we usually associate board games with indoor activities, in Africa they were played both indoors and outdoors, and depending on where you live or the time of year you may be able to do the same; and (2) There are so many fascinating games, and strategy activities were such an important part of African culture, that we thought this sampling deserved to be on its own. We emphasize that this is a sampling because strategy games can be found throughout Africa, and many closely resemble each other, so any game you see here was probably played, with variations, by people in different parts of the continent.

Generally, the games described below can be played by children of any age, though it will often be the case the players seven years old and under will need an adult partner. Also, we've simplified the way board games can be made so that they are easier and less expensive to create.

By the way, as you play these games, note how some of them closely resemble board games sold in stores. Ancient African games and their descendants played in this century have been adapted and issued by most of the major games manufacturers, usually with new titles. You might already have a few in your closet!

ACHI

Number of Players: 2
Age: 8 to 12
Equipment: Piece of white paper
Red and yellow construction paper
Pencil
Scissors

ORIGIN:

This is another game that, as far as we know, has no specific origin but was played in several African countries. An achi board was found carved into the roof of an Egyptian temple built over 3000 years ago, yet versions were also played in Sudan, Uganda, and Rwanda. In the United States today, there are similarities between Achi and Tic-Tac-Toe.

HOW TO PLAY:

1. On the white piece of paper, draw two lines, each connecting two corners. Then draw two lines that separate the paper into four squares. You should now have a total of eight lines that all connect in the center of the paper.

2. Using the construction paper, cut out four small yellow circles and four small red circles. These are your playing pieces. (If you have red and yellow playing pieces from any other source, these are fine.)

3. Players take turns putting pieces on points of the board (there are nine in all) where two or more lines intersect.

4. With all the pieces on the board, the object is for each player to move his pieces to try to get three in a row lined up, in any direction.

5. Players can move pieces in any way, from one point to the next or jumping to another point. Part of the play will be "defensive," trying to prevent your opponent from lining up three in a row. At the same time, though, you're trying to get your own pieces lined up.

6. The first player to line up three pieces is the winner.

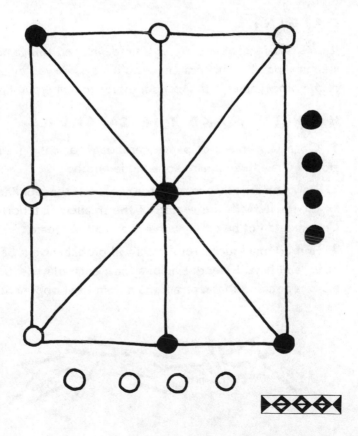

ATI DADA
("Little Sticks")

Number of Players: 2
Age: 8 to 12
Equipment: Paper, cardboard, or oaktag
Pencil or pen
Toothpicks

ORIGIN:

It isn't certain what country or tribe developed this game. There are many possibilities, because as you'll see when you try out some of the other games in this section, there are numerous similarities.

HOW TO MAKE THE BOARD:

1. On a large piece of paper, cardboard, or oaktag, or in the ground, draw three squares, one inside another.

2. Draw four lines that connect the centers of the four lines of the largest square with the centers of the smallest (interior) square. Lines should not be drawn within the smallest square.

3. Find 20 small sticks. Toothpicks will probably work best. Each player will have 10, and it helps a lot if each player's sticks have markers or colors that separate them from their opponent's sticks.

HOW TO PLAY:

1. Two players sit opposite each other. Taking turns, they place their sticks extending out from the points where lines connect.

2. When all 20 sticks have been put down, players take turns moving the sticks to an unoccupied point. You can't move the same stick twice in a row.

3. The object is for a player to line up three of her sticks in a row so they form (or come close to forming) a consecutive line. Strategy is important because not only must you try to line up your own sticks, but you have to move your sticks to prevent your opponent from lining up three of her sticks in consecutive order.

4. Every time three sticks are lined up, you can remove one of your opponent's sticks. When you have captured all the sticks or effectively blocked a player from moving, you win.

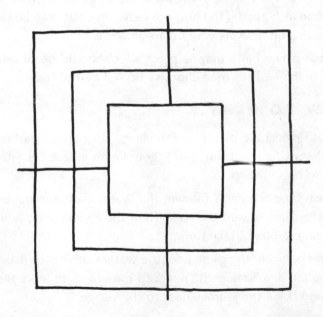

HYENA CHASE

ORIGIN:

This game is not attributed to any specific country, but was a favorite among people who lived in the northern part of Africa. You will need a die to throw to play this game.

HOW TO MAKE THE BOARD:

1. On or in any surface, draw a circle that represents a water well. Then, off in one corner, draw a larger circle that represents a village.

2. Spiraling out from the well, draw four rings, with the outer ring leading to the village. Then on these rings, draw small circles about an inch apart. (The distance between circles can be smaller, depending on how big your board surface is.)

3. Each player has a playing piece which should be of different color or shape. They then choose who will be the Hyena.

HOW TO PLAY:

1. Both pieces are placed in the village. The Water Gatherer, or the player who is not the Hyena, goes first — in fact, he gets three turns to begin the game.

2. Each time the die is thrown, the Water Gatherer moves from circle to circle toward the well. Then the Hyena goes, and from then on the players take turns.

3. One object of the game is for the Water Gatherer to make it to the well. When he does, he needs to throw a six to leave the well area and begin the journey back to the village.

4. On the way back, any time either player throws a six, he gets to go again.

5. The second object of the game is to arrive safely back in the village, with water and without being eaten by the Hyena. To add excitement at the finish, the Water Gatherer needs to roll the die so that he lands exactly in the village. To be fair, the Hyena also needs to roll the exact number of spaces to "pounce" on his victim.

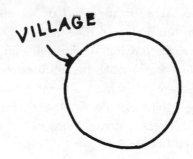

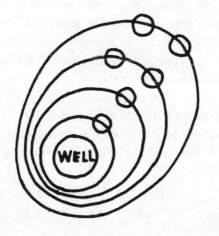

MANKALA

ORIGIN:

It is difficult to report with certainty when and where this game was created because it was played just about everywhere in Africa. One source contends that the most popular version of Mankala was developed in the court of Shamba of the Bonnet, who was ruler of the Bushongo tribe in the Congo. He was well known for his peacekeeping efforts, for being an inventor, and for extensive traveling. Supposedly, he returned from a trip to Egypt with a board game called Mankala, and he tinkered with it before introducing it to his people. Another source says that the game did not originate in any part of Africa but was brought to the continent from the Middle East.

A version of the game was played in Sierra Leone, though there only royalty was allowed to play. In West Africa the game was known as Owari. Elsewhere in Africa, the game is called Wari, Awari, or Mancala. Whatever the title, the game is basically the same. The Mankala board could be sophisticated and ornate, some even of gold or other precious metals. And Mankala boards have been found carved into stone in the pyramid of Cheops and the temples of Luxor and Karnak in Egypt.

However, one reason for the game's popularity is that the board is easy to make with readily available materials, so people young and old, rich or poor, and in any region could play it.

HOW TO MAKE THE BOARD:

1. Take an empty egg carton, cut off the top, and put it aside. And, be sure to snip off the tops of the columns that separate the eggs.

2. Take a flat piece of wood — it can be only a half-inch thick but should be longer than the egg carton — and glue the bottom of the egg carton top onto it. Place the other part of the egg carton within this base.

3. On the lengthwise sides of the egg carton, glue two paper cups. It's best if they're short ones, or cut the cups down to two to three inches tall.

4. Now you can get a little bit fancy. Using four or six short pieces of tape, secure the egg carton top to the base. Then you can cover the base with papier-mâché, and when it dries paint the base.

5. Collect forty playing pieces, called *hasa*, of the same size. Small marbles or beads will work fine.

HOW TO PLAY:

1. Two players sit on opposite sides (across the length) of the board, so that each has a cup in front.

2. The first player takes the forty hasa and drops them into the twelve holes — at least two but no more than five in each hole.

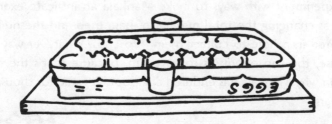

3. The second player, beginning with the right-hand hole on her side, picks up all the hasa in it. Then, continuing around to the right, she drops one hasa into each hole until all she collected has been dropped. If the number of hasa in the last hole is two or four, she takes all the hasa in the hole opposite it. Those hasa are placed in that player's cup. (If the last hole didn't contain two or four hasa, the turn ends and the other player repeats the process.)

4. After dropping the hasa into her cup, the second player returns to the last hole, picks up the hasa, and again, moving to the right, drops one into each hole. Her turn ends when she drops one into an empty hole or the last hole she dropped a hasa in doesn't contain two or four pieces.

5. The first player, beginning with his right-hand hole, performs the procedure, placing any collected hasa into his cup. As the game continues, if the right-hand hole is empty to begin a turn, start with the next hole to the right that contains hasa.

6. The game ends when too few hasa remain to collect pieces. The players count up the hasa in their cups, and the winner is the one with the most pieces.

This is a simplified version of Mankala. As you can imagine, since there are several versions played by people across an entire continent, Mankala games could be more complicated. You may wish to experiment with ways to make Mankala an intricate exercise, such as changing the total number of hasa used and the number required in a hole to collect them into cups. Whatever way you choose, the top priority is to have fun, because that's the main reason why Mankala has endured as a popular game for thousands of years.

MURABARABA

ORIGIN:

This game originates from one of the smallest countries in Africa. Lesotho is surrounded by South Africa. Young shepherds invented it as they sat in fields or on hillsides keeping an eye on their flocks.

HOW TO MAKE THE BOARD:

1. In the ground or on a large piece of paper/cardboard/oaktag, draw a large square. Inside it, maybe three inches apart, draw another square. Then inside that one, about six inches apart, draw a third square.

2. Draw lines to connect the corners of the two outer squares. Also, draw two long lines that connect the centers of the outer square.

3. Wherever lines connect, draw a small circle. You should have a total of 25 small circles

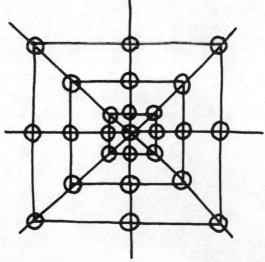

HOW TO PLAY:

1. Two players or teams sit on opposite sides of the board. Each has 12 small playing pieces, which can be stones or beans. One group of pieces should be a different color from the other.

2. Use any fun method to determine who goes first. One at a time, the players place their pieces on open circles.

3. The object is for a player to place pieces so that three consecutive circles are covered. This formation is called a "strike." When one player makes a strike, she can remove one piece belonging to the other player from the board. If you happen to create two strikes by the addition of one piece, you can remove two opponent's pieces.

4. Once all the pieces have been put down, the players take turns moving them, trying to make more strikes. You must move from one connected circle to another, no jumping.

5. The losing player has only two pieces left, and is thus unable to make a strike, or is blocked from removing any of her remaining pieces.

SEEGA

ORIGIN:

This game is sometimes called Egyptian Checkers because it originated in the village of Silwa in the southern part of Egypt.

HOW TO MAKE THE BOARD:

1. On any suitable surface, draw a large square. Then, within the
square, draw four equidistant lines connecting the top and bottom and four more connecting the other two sides.

2. You should have 25 square boxes. Find 24 small objects of two
colors — coins can work well, using heads and tails — that will be
divided equally between two players.

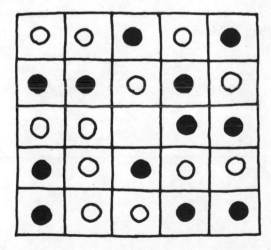

HOW TO PLAY:

1. Choose who will make the first move. That player places two of his pieces in any squares except the center one.

2. The players then take turns putting their pieces down. When they're done, only the center square will be unoccupied.

3. The player who went second last time goes first this time and moves one piece — obviously, it has to be into the center square. As the moves continue, pieces can be moved only in adjacent empty squares.

4. The strategy is to place two pieces on either side of an opponent's piece, which is removed. The winner is the player who captures all of his opponent's pieces (or whose opponent is blocked and cannot move).

There is a variation of this game called Kei or "Sierra Leone checkers" that is played with 100 squares and 40 pieces. It is much more complicated, and thus was played more by teenagers and adults rather than children.

SEY

ORIGIN:

The Dogon tribe of Mali is the inventor of this game. It originated from a tribal myth that at the beginning of the world, when the earth and sky were closer together, Dogon parents plucked stars from the sky as toys for their children. That such "hide and seek" games were common among many peoples of Africa implies that this myth was part of other tribes too.

HOW TO MAKE THE BOARD:

1. It seems that this game was always played outdoors, so there isn't exactly a board. In the ground, draw two circles, one within another and about three inches apart.

2. Two players sit opposite each other, and in a space on their side between the two circles they dig three small holes.

3. A *tibi*, or a very small object, probably a pebble, is used.

HOW TO PLAY:

1. The first player, the one chosen to conceal the tibi, gathers loose dirt in her hand. Moving from left to right, she trickles dirt into the three holes, secretly dropping the tibi into one of them.

2. After this is done, the opponent calls, "*Deny, deny!*" which in the Dogon language means, "Come out, come out!" She then has one guess to pick the hole containing the tibi. If she is incorrect, the first player digs an additional hole and goes again, but he can't drop the tibi into the same hole. If she is correct, it's her turn.

3. The players take turns, each allowed to dig another hole for every one of her opponent's incorrect answers, moving left to right around the space between the circles.

4. The first player to reach the opponent's hole is the winner.

SHISIMA
("Source of Water")

ORIGIN:

You'll be reminded of Tic-Tac-Toe when you play this game from Kenya. Invention of the game is attributed to the Tutriki tribe who watched *imbalavali*, or beetle-like insects, crawling toward water.

HOW TO MAKE THE BOARD:

1. In the ground or on a large piece of paper, draw a circle, which represents a pool of water, in the center.

2. Draw eight straight lines out from the center, and then draw lines to connect the ends of those lines. The shape should represent an octagon.

3. At the three top points and the three bottom points, place beans or rocks to represent insects.

HOW TO PLAY:

1. Each player or team sits behind its three insects.

2. Taking turns, each player moves an insect to an adjacent vacant line. Each piece is allowed three moves before moving into the pool.

3. The first player to get all three insects into the pool wins. Does this sound too easy? It isn't: When you play, you'll see that strategy is involved.

YOTE

ORIGIN:

This was a popular strategy game in West Africa. The version most often played today comes from Senegal. Perhaps you can find a way to create a "board," but this was an outdoor game.

HOW TO MAKE THE BOARD:

1. In the ground, dig out five rows of six small holes each.

2. Find 24 small playing pieces, usually twigs or pebbles.

HOW TO PLAY:

1. Two players, each with 12 playing pieces, sit on opposite sides of the dug-out "boards."

2. The first player places a pebble in a hole; then the second player does the same.

3. Here's where the strategy begins: With each turn, a player can choose to drop in another pebble or move a pebble already in a hole. To capture an opponent's pebble, you must jump over it "straight," not diagonally. Obviously, if a jump isn't available, your move is to add another pebble.

4. The object is to capture all the opponent's pebbles or to create a situation where the opponent is unable to move without being captured. However, unlike many other games, it's possible for Yote to end in a tie.

This game is especially fun when teams play, because each team can be allowed one minute to discuss strategy before moving a pebble.

CRAFT-MAKING
ACTIVITIES

This section's format is a bit different, because creating a craft object can be done by a single youngster or by a group, so "number of players" doesn't apply here. Also, determining the ability to make any of the objects in this section is subjective. Generally, these crafts are appropriate for older children, but a particular seven-year-old may be just as capable as a ten-year-old, and in most cases — around the kitchen table or in an afterschool program or day-care center — adult participation can enable any youngster to perform the activity.

Since the purpose of the activity is to have fun and to create a craft, everybody is a "winner." The activities in this section offer minutes or hours of education and pleasure, and the effort is its own reward. A suggestion to parents and other caregivers: Creating some of the crafts requires the use of knives, scissors, or other tools, so it is a good idea to decide beforehand the extent of adult supervision.

Probably every culture in the world has produced crafts. They can widely vary, but the purposes are the same — to create something useful or decorative. People in Africa made crafts that could be used in their everyday lives for work or at home, and some items were placed around their homes simply because they were attractive additions. Skills were passed down from one generation to another, yet every child makes his/her own special craft.

As you'll discover, however closely you follow these directions, what you create will be unique. Like snowflakes, no two crafts are exactly alike.

To describe how to make every craft associated with African culture would require a book the size of a major city's telephone directory. For that reason, we have chosen to feature a sampling of crafts, ones that vary in origin, design, and the ability necessary to make them. There are books available — for example, *African Crafts You Can Make* and *Children Are Children Are Children* — that offer designs to make dozens of crafts, and you may want to look for them in your local bookstore or library.

Also, you may want to refer to this section after you read all about Kwanzaa later in this book. Making crafts is one of the more enjoyable activities during the seven-day observance of this special holiday, and you can take advantage of some of the descriptions here.

ADIRE ELESO

Materials: Broomstick cut into several pieces • Dye •
Bucket • White sheet • Plastic bag • String
or clothesline • Needle and thread

ORIGIN:

In Nigeria, *adire* is the name of a tie-dying process that produces
attractive patterns on cloth. Often the deep-blue dye made from
indigo plants was used. Here, any blue dye is fine, because blue is
a popular color for Nigerian clothing (it reduces the glare of sunlight); but other colors and combinations can be used.

HOW TO MAKE IT:

1. Wrap a piece of sheet around the stick, securing it with string.
If you wish some of the sheet to remain white, tie strips of plastic
around it.

2. In a bucket, make a solution of water and dye.

3. Dip the tied sheet into the bucket. The longer you leave it in
the dye the deeper the color will be, but usually three minutes is
plenty of time.

4. Lift up the stick and let the solution drip off. Cut the strings
and rinse the cloth in cold water.

5. Dry the cloth on clothesline, then smooth it out. (An adult can use an iron.)

6. Repeat the process using the same dye, then using different dyes.

7. You now have several sheets of cloth that are blue and white or of several colors. If you choose to sew them together, you can have a beautiful cape or shawl or a banner . . . or you can mix and match them any way you choose to create eye-catching patterns.

AKUABA
("Ashanti Doll")

Materials: Balsa wood • Beads • Macaroni •
Carving knife • Fishing weight •
Needle and thread • Glue • Paint •
Food coloring

ORIGIN:

In addition to the Ashanti tribe, these objects were created by members of the Yoruba tribe (who called them *Ibeji*). Ashanti women carried the dolls inside their clothing, near their waist, in the hope that they would give birth to beautiful, healthy children. Yoruba women had a different purpose. If one of a pair of twin babies died, a doll was created and cared for as the baby would have been, implying that this particular craft was used to help deal with grief.

HOW TO MAKE IT:

1. Take a six-inch piece of balsa wood about one inch in diameter and carve three indentations at one end, which will be the top, so that three neck rings are formed.

2. For the base, use a piece of wood about two inches in diameter and one inch high. Carve a hole in the top of the base large enough to contain the fishing weight.

3. For the two arms, use pieces of wood each about a half inch in diameter and three inches long.

4. The head should be about five inches in diameter but only about a quarter-inch thick. Cut two tiny holes on both sides of the head, about even with where the mouth will be.

5. You can carve features into the face, but it may be easier and more fun to create the features separately and then glue them on. You can use pieces of wood, papier-mâché, macaroni, or any other small, suitable objects, and if you wish color them with paint or food coloring.

6. Glue the pieces together — body atop base, arms to body, head on neck. Once the glue has dried, you can paint the doll if you haven't already painted the individual pieces.

7. Soak macaroni, enough to make an eighteen-inch string, in food coloring (tubettini works well). When the pieces are dry, run a string through them and tie the ends together. This is wrapped several times around the bottom of the body so it rests atop the base. You can then repeat this procedure with a shorter string of macaroni to go around the neck. (Make sure this string is wide enough to fit over the head!)

8. Thread a needle and push it through a few beans or small beads. Push one end of the strings through each of the tiny holes in the head, tie the ends, and you have earrings. Your Ashanti Doll is now complete.

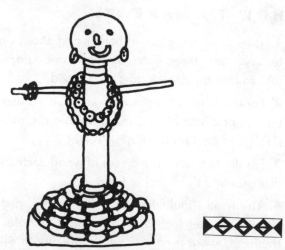

BASONGE BELL

Materials: Wood (2 pieces, each 1 inch thick) • Coping saw or jigsaw • Carving knife (or drill) • String • Clothespin (wooden) • Glue • Sandpaper

ORIGIN:

Many tribes in Africa made bells, for a variety of reasons — used in ceremonies, as house decorations, parts of necklaces, for cattle and dogs to wear, even musical instruments. For example, people of the Watusi tribe crafted small round bells and wore them around their ankles during dances. The bell you're about to make is from the Basonge tribe of the Congo.

HOW TO MAKE IT:

1. With the saw, cut out the inner shape of the bell, with a small "hump" at the top for the handle.

2. Drill or carve out the handle hole.

3. For the sides, cut two pieces of quarter-inch wood to fit the shape so that the sides will "sandwich" the middle.

4. To make a clapper, cut a two-inch piece from a clothespin. Drill or cut a small hole in the top of the clapper, then tie a string through it. Tie the clapper to the arch underneath the handle of the inner shape.

5. Now glue all three pieces together (the first shape you carved in the middle) so that the bell is formed.

6. If you want, you can sand down any rough edges of the bell.

7. Basonge bells usually had designs on both sides, often special ones that represented specific tribes or families. You can do the same by carving or, if you prefer, use paints to create designs.

CALABASH

Materials: Newspaper • Balloons • White glue and water •
Bowl • Sandpaper • Pin • Paint and shellac

ORIGIN:

This object is associated with Nigeria. A calabash was a decorative
item, yet they were also used to store water if an opening was left
at the top. A real calabash grows on a vine like a pumpkin or water-
melon, and a craftsman would scoop out the soft inside, then
harden the remaining half shells, often by simply leaving them out
in hot sunlight, sometimes by baking them. Since they don't grow
in North America, here's a way to create your own.

HOW TO MAKE THEM:

1. Tear newspaper into thin strips.

2. Blow up a few balloons. (The sizes depends on how big or small
you want your calabashes to be.)

3. Dip the strips of paper (after shaking off excess liquid) into a
bowl of mixed glue and water, then cover each balloon with several layers of sticky paper.

4. Let dry for a few hours. If there are rough edges, you can sand
them down. Do some extra sanding to form a flat base at the bottom.

5. Carefully using a pin, pop each balloon.

6. You can apply shellac, but even better is to paint the outside in
different colors. Try a different design for each calabash. Very nice!

CEREMONIAL MASK

Materials: Popsicle stick or wooden ruler • Paper plate •
Egg carton • Aluminum foil • Anything else
you can think of!

ORIGIN:

The people of many African tribes and countries created ceremonial masks. One of the best-known masks comes from Nigeria. There, people made masks to wear during religious worship ceremonies, and what makes them special is they often had exaggerated features — large mouths with many teeth (sometimes fangs), big noses, bulging eyes, wide ears, etc. As you'll see, masks allow for a lot of creativity!

HOW TO MAKE THEM:

1. With glue or by stapling, attach a stick to the paper plate (so it looks like a large lollipop).

2. Again using glue, affix objects resembling the features of a face to the plate, and try to be three-dimensional. For example, two paper cups can be the eyes, or one can be the nose. Shape aluminum foil like ears, or a long strip can be the mouth.

3. Before attaching anything, you can paint items — the brighter the better! Pieces of egg carton can be used for a beard or hair. This is one of those crafts that can look more friendly or fierce depending on how many materials you use, their variety, and where you place them.

CHAD HOUSE

Materials: Styrofoam • Clay • Coffee can • Glue •
Straw • Paint • Thin wooden pole •
Small sticks or toothpicks • String •
Pipe cleaners • Sharp knife • Papier-mâché

ORIGIN:

People in different parts of Africa built different kinds of houses, which had little to do with a family's preference. The deciding factor was usually the climate. People who lived in an area that had harsh or frequent rains built their houses with sloped or conical roofs so the rain wouldn't collect atop the house, threatening to collapse the roof, and also placed their houses (and sometimes their entire yards) on a small hill so that the rain would wash down and away. People who lived in very hot climates included many windows for cross-ventilation, and some even had a small roof, one not large enough to cover the entire house, supported by vertical poles. This allowed air to circulate, offered shade in the middle of the day, and cover the few times it did rain.

Another factor was protection. To give them options in case of attack, some "houses" were constructed as separate though usually connected compartments or rooms, so that if one part caught on fire or was otherwise damaged, other parts of the house would survive. Other considerations were crops or livestock. To store food, either to be eaten by the family or eventually sold, a connected structure could be designated for storage. The same is true for animals, which could be housed in the equivalent of a barn. Even when livestock wasn't kept indoors, a house could be separate yet connected buildings forming an open courtyard where at night the animals could roam and be better protected from predators.

Here is described how to make one kind of house, but there were other ones found throughout Africa. A house of the N'Debele tribe had a conical roof and was built at one end of a rectangular courtyard separated into sections for use by family members, especially for playing children and to do chores, for livestock, and for guests.

The people of Kano, a city in Nigeria which bordered the Sahara Desert, built houses and enclosed courtyards without roofs. The Nuba tribe in the Sudan built small cottages (with round, not rectangular doors) connected by curved walls, each conical roof adorned with a wooden or clay globe. It's likely that any variation of model house you choose to make (perhaps requiring more or different materials than the ones listed above) will have a counterpart somewhere in Africa.

Most of the people who lived around Lake Chad were fishermen and farmers. Their houses were round and made of mud, with straw or "rushes" forming the conical roofs.

HOW TO MAKE IT:

1. Take an empty coffee can and remove its bottom. Then, starting from the bottom, cut out a small rectangle for a door. Wrap the can in papier-mâché, making sure to retain the door opening.

2. Paint the exterior of the can. A tan or light-brown color is best.

3. Cover the top of a half-inch-thick piece of Styrofoam with a thin layer of clay. Before the clay dries, press the coffee can into the center of the piece of Styrofoam so that the latter is the base or foundation. Plant the thin wooden pole in the clay in the base within the can so that it extends straight up above the rim. Also plant in a circle outside the bottom of the can about a dozen small sticks or toothpicks.

4. Cut out a piece of woven straw from a beach hat or bag with a diameter slightly larger than that of the top of the can. Wet the straw so that it is more flexible and affix it to the pole so that its edges rest on the circular top of the can.

5. Gently connect the tops of the sticks with pipe cleaners.

6. Cut strips of woven straw in lengths that will extend between two sticks.

7. Attach the straw segments by weaving in and around pieces of string between sticks. This will form a fence around the house, creating an exterior yard.

8. For extra realism, take some clay and make small clay pots, maybe 2 inches high, to place next to the house (they were used to collect rainwater) and against one part of the fence stack some short sticks to represent a woodpile. There are probably other items you can think of to help this house look more like the real home of someone who lived near the shores of Lake Chad.

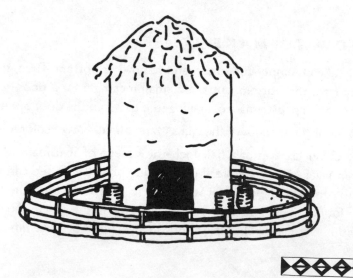

CORN NECKLACE

Materials: Thin cardboard • Dried corn husk with dried kernels • Glue • Hole puncher • Scissors • Different-colored yarns

ORIGIN:

This craft really can't be associated with a specific country. Necklaces used for various ceremonies, barter, or money, or just for decoration were made throughout Africa.

HOW TO MAKE IT:

1. Cut five corn shapes from the cardboard.

2. Punch two holes in the top (or wider part) of each shape.

3. Take three pieces of yarn of different colors and weave them in and out of the holes to form a necklace. Tie the ends of the yarn together.

4. Glue a piece of corn husk at the top of each shape. Then cover the outer side of each corn shape with glue.

5. Pick off dried kernels from the real corn husk and place them on the corn shapes, covering much of each surface. When the glue dries, you have an attractive, colorful necklace. For more variety of colors, feel free to paint the kernels.

KUFI

Materials: Light-colored construction paper (12 by 18 inches) • Small sponge • Paper plate • Three colors of paint • Pencil • Glue • Scissors • Stapler

ORIGIN:

In many parts of Africa, men wear a hat known as a *kufi*. It can be part of a ceremony or just worn to display African heritage.

HOW TO MAKE IT:

1. Cut the sponge into three small rectangles.

2. Dip the sponge pieces into the paints and then make impressions on the construction paper to form a pattern of different colors.

3. When the paint has dried, place the paper plate face down at one end of the construction paper, then use the pencil to trace a line around it.

4. Cut the circle out. Then cut two bands from the rest of the paper and staple the ends together.

5. Glue the circle of the construction paper to the bottom side of the plate.

6. Staple the bands, painted side outward, to the "crown" of the hat.

7. You now have a *kufi*. For bigger heads, you may have to decorate and cut bands from an extra piece of construction paper.

PORO MASK

Materials: Paper plate • Cardboard • Scissors or carving knife • Papier-mâché (paste, paper, and water) • Paints • Aluminum foil • Glue or household cement • Cotton balls • Nylon stocking • Needle and thread • Clay • Thin wire, string, or fishing line • Thread • Metal bolts • Thin rope

ORIGIN:

Of course, many African masks were made to be worn in front of a person's face or entirely over the head. Sometimes, though, masks were created not to be worn but to be carried atop a pole (they could be unusually large) or to hang on a belt or necklace (they were small). Though masks were occasionally designed for use in battle — fierce-looking ones to frighten enemies — in most cases masks were an important part of religious ceremonies. In the Dan tribe of Liberia there was a male-only organization known as the Poro Society that worshiped the tribe's ancestors through ceremonial dances that included masks.

HOW TO MAKE IT:

1. Take a paper plate and glue onto it a nose and a mouth that could be pieces of cardboard, wood, or Styrofoam. Make sure to provide nostrils in the nose.

2. Cover the plate with papier-mâché, but make sure that the nose and mouth aren't covered. Also, cut two wide slits in the papier-mâché for eyes, and two small holes on either side of the mask. If you want to, as the papier-mâché dries gently curve the plate at the sides so that later you have the option of actually wearing the mask and it will better conform to the contours of your face.

3. When the papier-mâché is dry, paint the mask. Don't hesitate to use bright colors!

4. Cut aluminum foil into two pieces large enough to cover the eyes and curl up on top to form eyebrows. Glue them into position. You can also ball up small pieces of foil and glue them into the mouth for teeth.

5. For the headpiece, cut a piece of nylon stocking, stuff it with cotton balls, sew it together so it becomes a cotton-ball-filled tube, and glue it around the top of the mask so that the edges come down to where ears would be.

6. Take colored beads and glue them under the chin and then around on both sides until they meet up with the headpiece.

7. Using two pieces of the thin wire, string, or fishing line, push one edge through one of the holes on either side of the mask. On these pieces can be strung beads or even metal bolts that will represent long earrings. The more varied the colors the better, though the bolts are fun because of the jangling sound they will make.

8. If you want to wear the mask (it might be a bit heavy), thread string through the two available holes on either side of the mask and tie the ends. The mask can now fit securely over your face, and you can breathe through the nostrils.

9. If you want to use the mask for decoration, thread a smaller piece of string or thin wire through the two available holes. The mask can then be suspended close to a wall from a nail.

SHIELDS

Materials: Two kite sticks (30 inches each) • Stick (11 inches long) • Glue • Papier-mâché • (paste, paper, and water) • String • Newspaper • Plastic bleach bottle • Scissors or carving knife • Paints • Fake fur fabric • Clothespins • Yarn

ORIGIN:

A shield was an important symbol in African culture. Each tribe produced its own shield. There were some variations, but one could identify the tribe by seeing its shield. It had a practical purpose in combat, to protect the warrior carrying the shield. But shields were also used in dances and religious ceremonies. The one you make can reflect your own tastes in colors and patterns. Here you can make a shield from the Masai tribe of Kenya, though one with a round shape could easily resemble a shield from the Zulu tribe of South Africa.

HOW TO MAKE THE SHIELD:

1. At the centers, connect with glue the two longer kite sticks with the shorter one. It's probably a good idea to reinforce the holding power of the glue by tightly wrapping the connecting points with twine or tape.

2. Across this frame wrap string about a dozen times, top to bottom. Leave the string a bit loose.

3. Now cover one side of the frame with papier-mâché, the wrapped string helping to form a foundation. Immediately after doing this, stick a small piece of wood, plastic bleach bottle, or some other buffer between the middle of the center stick and the papier-mâché. Before the papier-mâché is completely dry, remove this buffer so you have a handle you can grasp behind the shield.

4. Get out the paints! The decoration of the shield's surface is completely up to you. Keep in mind, though, that certain color combinations are best if you want the shield's appearance to be fierce, funny, or just an interesting design.

5. The shield can be hung on a wall by hanging the top (whichever end you choose to be the top!) on a nail. Or, if you want to carry it around, the space between the center piece and the papier-mâché provides a handle.

MUSICAL GAMES

By learning about cultures around the world, one can appreciate the different ways music and dance were used — for education, entertainment, worship, or to prepare for battle. In Africa, music and dance were used for all of the above, and more.

Being such a large continent with so many countries, cities, villages, tribes, and distinct geographic areas, it is very hard (and probably inaccurate) to make generalizations about Africa . . . except, perhaps, about music and dance. These were extremely important parts of the culture. Physical movement and accompanying music (including chants) were ways for one generation to pass to the next a variety of skills and knowledge, and sometimes for entire communities to share fun.

Games that incorporate music and dance were popular among children and encouraged by adults. It would be impossible to fit into one book all of the musical games that originated in Africa, but here we offer a sampling that conveys some favorite activities and ones that can be easily learned by youngsters. Especially pleasurable were music and dance games and ceremonies played or practiced by adults and children — we hope you do the same with these examples.

In all the games, the number of players can vary, and often the more the merrier . . . if there is room! They can be played outdoors or indoors. There is no need to use real instruments; readily available materials can be used or combined to create a fine sound. The age of players usually doesn't matter, especially if adults are participating. The scenarios and movements are basic ones, and the lyrics are not complicated. Indeed, if some youngsters are so inclined, once they are comfortable with the games they can invent their own appropriate lyrics and experiment with different movements. There really is no "right" way to enjoy a music-and-dance game, and certainly no winners and losers. Following are general guidelines that can evolve into games reflecting your own taste, modes of expression, and sense of fun.

A-FISHING

Equipment: Long rope

Chalk or natural markers

ORIGIN:

This game comes from Ghana and is also associated with Togo. It's likely that variations of it were played in countries that bordered water.

HOW TO PLAY:

1. A player is selected to be a Fisherman.

2. A portion of the playing area is marked off so that it is considered a river, lake, or ocean.

3. The Fisherman holds the rope that represents a net.

4. The other players pretend to swim in the water, approaching and then retreating from the Fisherman standing on the shore.

5. As the Fisherman sings a song, she wades into the water. As she begins to sing the last line of the song, she tries to catch fish by encircling as many as she can with the rope. A player or players caught within the rope are brought back to shore.

6. The game continues as there are more Fishermen trying to catch fish. The last fish swimming free becomes the Fisherman in the next game.

SONG:

We come, we come! We come, we come!
We are fishermen. We come out a-fishing, oh!
We come out a-fishing, oh!
Haul the fish in, catch them so!

Yea-b'o, yea-b'o! Yea-b'o, yea-b'o!
Ye-yea-fare-fo. Ye-baa mpa-taa-yi, mon-hwe!
Ye-baa mpa-taa-yi, mon-hwe!
Se-nea yek-yere won, mon-hwe!

CHA CHA KOFI SA

Equipment: None

ORIGIN:

This singing game from Ghana is fun for children of any age. It can get really silly, because as it is played, the more nonsense syllables, the better!

HOW TO PLAY:

1. One player is selected to play the role of leader. She stands before the others, who imitate what she does and sings.

2. Rocking from one foot to the other, the leader sings, "Cha cha koo lay."

3. Placing her hands on her head, she sings, "Cha cha ko fi sa."

4. Placing fingertips on shoulders, she sings, "Ko fi sa lan gee."

5. Hands on her knees, she sings, "Cum a den dee."

6. The leader then goes back to the beginning and repeats the motions and singing the lines. Every time she starts from the beginning, she goes faster, with the group trying to keep up.

7. When she's ready, the leader abruptly ends the game by crumpling to the floor or ground.

8. Two ways to add to the fun:

    a. Substitute nonsense syllables or words (nice ones!) that will get a laugh.

    b. When the group also crumples to the ground, the last one down is out. Continue playing until only one member of the group is left, who becomes the leader for the next game.

CHINENE NYE?
("What Is Big?")

Equipment: None

ORIGIN:

Played by the people of the Ovimbundu tribe, this game comes from the country now called Zimbabwe.

HOW TO PLAY:

1. A player is chosen as the song leader, and the other players are the chorus.

2. This is a "call and response" activity, meaning that for every question or command the leader offers, the chorus answers back, forming a chant.

> **Leader:** *Chinene nye?* ("What is big?")
>
> **Chorus:** *Chinene onjamba.* ("Elephant is big.")
>
> **Leader:** *Chinene nye?*
>
> **Chorus:** *Chinene onjamba.* ("Elephant is big.")
>
> *Kinyama viosi.* ("Among all the animals of the world.")
>
> *Ka ku li ukuavo.* ("There is none larger.")

3. After the players repeat this stanza, the leader chooses another animal, and then another, offering animals that can generally be considered big. Some examples are:

> *Malanga:* Cheetah
> *Ngeve:* Hippopotamus
> *Hosi:* Lion
> *Ngue:* Leopard

Obviously, if the African names aren't used, more animal names are available to call out. The chorus responds the same way as it did with the other animals.

4. Now the leader can have fun. He can choose to call out the name of an animal not considered big, such as "Crab" or "Kitten" or "Mouse." These names should be mixed up with other or repeated large animals.

5. Players who respond incorrectly — for example, "Mouse is big" — are out, so chorus members have to be on their toes.

6. The last player remaining calls, *O wi* ("Song ends") and becomes the song leader in the next game.

FOLLOW THE LEADER

Equipment: None

ORIGIN:

The game's name indicates that versions are played around the world. However, this particular version comes from the Gabon Pygmies, people known for their short stature — though youngsters of any size can play! Also, this is more of an activity than a game because the only goal is to laugh.

HOW TO PLAY:

1. One player is chosen to begin. She stands up in front of the others and by movement and facial expressions imitates a bird or animal.

2. As she mimics the animals, she chants:

> *A horse does . . . snort, neigh, jump!*
> *A bird goes . . . (imitate a bird)*
> *A fish does . . . (imitate a fish)*

3. The other players stand to quickly imitate what the first player is doing. (It doesn't matter how well they copy.) The first player can continue as long as she wants, but to give everyone a fair chance it's probably a good idea to set a limit, say five animals.

4. Other players take turns. Again, there is no winner, but it adds to the fun for players to (a) imitate animals not mentioned before, and (b) try to make their imitations as outlandish as possible. If the activity is successful, players will be convulsed with laughter . . . and it is especially hilarious when adults participate.

GO TELL AUNT NANCY

Equipment: Three scarves of different colors

ORIGIN:

This particular version comes from the Hausa tribe of West Africa. "Aunt Nancy," however, is a derivation of Anansi, a spider that is a very popular fictional creature in the Caribbean and South America as well as Africa. She is known for her intelligence and cleverness. To keep this game to a reasonable length of time, it's best to play it with ten or a dozen children.

HOW TO PLAY:

1. One player is chosen to be Aunt Nancy and wears one colored scarf, another is chosen to be the Fox and wears a different scarf, and a third is chosen to be Mother Goose and wears the last scarf. The remaining players are Mother Goose's goslings.

2. Mother Goose and the goslings sit on the floor or ground. Fox hides in his "den." Aunt Nancy tells the group that Fox is around, so watch out for themselves because she has to go off on an errand. Aunt Nancy leaves.

3. Fox appears. He uses some excuse to get Mother Goose to follow him to his den. The goslings stand and form a circle and chant:

> Go tell Aunt Nancy,
> That poor Mother Goose is gone.
> She left nine [or seven] little goslings
> All alone.

4. Aunt Nancy returns, feigns being upset, and tells the goslings they must look out for themselves. After she leaves, Fox reappears and persuades a gosling to accompany him to his den. The remaining goslings stand and chant:

> *The Fox came and took one,*
> *Now there are eight [or six] alone.*

5. This is repeated over and over until there is only one gosling left. As she is being led away by Fox, she chants:

> *Who will tell Aunt Nancy*
> *That Fox took every one?*
> *And now there are* (loud) *none!*

6. With this, Aunt Nancy returns and hides. Mother Goose and her goslings chase Fox out of his den, and he is suddenly caught by Aunt Nancy.

JUBA THIS AND JUBA THAT

Equipment: None

ORIGIN:

For the most part, this rhyming game was developed by African Americans in the nineteenth century. Slave or free, many families had to eat whatever was available — leftovers, hand-picked vegetables, ends of meat and bread, "a little of this and a little of that" — and a way to make the meal tasty was to cook or mix all the different ingredients together to produce something new. *Juba* may be a variation of the word giblets, and for a while in New Orleans in the early 1800s there was a dance performed by African Americans called the Juba that used a variety of spontaneous movements. This version is reminiscent of that dance, with words added in the following decades.

HOW TO PLAY:

1. One person is chosen as the Caller, and the other players follow his made-up movements.

2. At the end of each first line, the players clap once. At the end of each second line, they clap twice.

3. The game can continue indefinitely — as long as the Caller can keep inventing rhymes. (For younger children, some allowances should be made for "close-enough" rhymes.) If he gets stuck, he is replaced by another player.

4. This traditional chant will get you going, but feel free to start off with your own.

> *Juba this and juba that,*
> *And Juba killed a yellow cat.*
> *You sift a meal, you give me the husk,*
> *You cook the bread, you give me the crust.*
> *You fry the meat, you give me the skin,*
> *And that's where my mama's troubles begin.*
> *Then you juba,*
> *You just juba.*
> *Juba up, juba down.*
> *Juba all around the town.*
> *Juba for ma, juba for pa,*
> *Juba for your brother-in-law.*
> *Juba that and juba this.*
> *I'll keep rhyming, I won't miss.*

KYE KYE KOLE

Equipment: None

ORIGIN:

This is a rather unusual, funny game from Ghana. Why is it unusual? Well, though the activity includes words to be sung, they aren't supposed to mean anything! In that case, of course, it doesn't matter what words are used and probably every group of children who played could just make up their own nonsense lyrics. The words offered here can be substituted for or changed any way you want, but apparently this version was the game most often played.

HOW TO PLAY:

1. Players stand in a circle, except for one chosen to be It, who stands in the center.

2. Putting hands on head, It sings, "*Che che kole.*" The other players do the same.

3. It sings another verse, making a different motion, such as hands on knees, and the other players follow along. This continues through the song.

4. When the song is finished, It falls to the ground, as do the others. Suddenly, It jumps up and tries to tag one of the other players, who have also risen and are running away. Whoever is tagged becomes It.

SONG:

Che che kole, che che kole.
Che che kofi sa che che kofi sa.
Kofi sa langa, kofi sa langa.
Ca-ca shi langa, ca-ca shi langa.
Koom ma dye day, koom ma dye day.

LITTLE SALLY WALKER

Equipment: None

ORIGIN:

Unlike most of the activities in this book, this game originated in the United States and has been played by African-American children. The song used is "Shake It to the One You Love the Best," the title of an excellent collection of songs and activities compiled by Cheryl Warren Mattox.

HOW TO PLAY:

1. Players form a ring around one child, who is Sally.

2. Sally kneels and sings the song, acting out its words. As she does this, the other players hold hands, move in a circle, and join the song.

3. As Sally sings "Shake it to the east . . ." she moves toward the players, feinting and retreating, until at the song's end she chooses one to replace her within the ring.

SONG:

Little Sally Walker sitting in a saucer,
Ride, Sally, ride.
Wipe your weeping eyes,
Put your hands on your hips,
And let your backbone slip.
Shake it to the east,
Shake it to the west,
Shake it to the one you love the best!

Little Sally Walker sitting in a saucer,
Crying for the old man to come for the dollar.
Ride, Sally, ride.
Put your hands on your hips
And let your backbone slip.
(Etc.)

MELON DANCE

Equipment: Soccer ball or volleyball

ORIGIN:

It might get kind of messy to use a melon in this game, which comes from South Africa. Music isn't involved, but a form of dance is.

HOW TO PLAY:

1. The players form a circle, with one youngster standing in the center holding the ball.

2. She runs, skips, and dances (or all of her movements can be considered an improvised dance) within the circle, all the while tossing up and catching the ball.

3. The surrounding players imitate her movements.

4. Suddenly the center player stops and rolls the ball backward between her feet. The player it comes to must catch it without moving from her position.

5. If she catches it, she takes her place in the center. If the ball isn't caught, the first player repeats her dance (or does a completely different routine).

6. To add to the fun, the center player can only pretend to roll the ball.

7. Though the center player can toss the ball at random, to be fair it's probably a good idea during the game to try to give every player a chance to catch it.

MY MAMA'S CALLING ME

Equipment: None

ORIGIN:

Like Little Sally Walker, this game was also developed in the African-American culture.

HOW TO PLAY:

1. The players form a circle around one youngster in the middle.

2. As the center player sings each verse, the other players respond by singing the second verse as a chorus.

3. During the song, the player in the center tries to leave the circle. Whoever lets her through takes her place in the middle.

SONG:

My mama's calling me.
You can't get out of here.
My mama's calling me.
You can't get out of here.
What shall I do?
Pat your ones to your knees.
What shall I do?
Pat your twos to your knees.

(Repeat until the center player escapes.)

NKOSI SIKELEL' I AFRIKA
("Prayer for Africa")

ORIGIN:

This isn't a game or an activity, but this short song is included here because of its interesting history and relevance to contemporary events in Africa.

The song was composed by a member of the Zulu tribe in South Africa in 1897 and was first performed in public, in the city of Johannesburg, two years later. The implication of its lyrics is that one day the country's native black residents would achieve equal rights with the white residents, many of whom were descendants of people who had emigrated from Great Britain and Holland. "Prayer for Africa" was regularly sung in schools reserved exclusively for black children, and its popularity spread to other parts of the country when the touring Ohlange Zulu Choir included it in their repertoire.

In the early part of this century the African National Congress was formed. Over the decades this organization worked hard to secure legal, economic, social, and other rights for black South Africans, and more recently to install a national government that reflected the country's black majority. Since the 1950s the most well-known member of the ANC has been Nelson Mandela, who advocated resistance to Apartheid, the policy that forced segregation between white people and people of color. For his efforts, Mandela spent nearly thirty years in prison.

Ironically, "Prayer for Africa" became so popular that it was viewed as a sort of national anthem and was sung at government ceremonies and other important events. But for the ANC, which adopted the song as its anthem, the song represented the dream of a desegregated country, one that promoted equality for all. That dream is becoming a reality. Soon after Mandela was released from prison in 1991, the white minority government stepped down and for the first time free elections — meaning every adult could vote — were held in South Africa. The result was a black majority government, with Mandela as President.

At his inauguration, all across the country millions of voices sang "Prayer for Africa."

Prayer for Africa

Bless, O Lord, our country, Africa,
So that she may waken from her sleep.
Fill her horn with plenty, guide her feet,
Hear us, faithful sons.
Come, spirit!

Nkosi, sikelel' i Afrika,
Malupakam' upondo lwayo.
Yiva imitandazo yetu,
Usisikelele.
Uje roho!

SIKILEKO

("Whistle for Me")

Equipment: None

ORIGIN:

Like What Is Big? on page 124, this game comes from Zimbabwe. It is very much like Hide and Seek, but with music.

HOW TO PLAY:

1. A player is selected to be It. He hides his face against a wall or tree.

2. The other players go off and hide as It counts to twenty-five.

3. It begins to look for the players. As he does, he sings a song:

> Cassossolo, cassossolo,
> Where did Pigeon cry from?
> He cried from the thicket.
> But the thicket is very, very quiet.
> Whistle for me! Whistle again!
>
> Cassossolo, cassossolo
> Nende wa lila pi?
> Wa lila ve tete.
> Va tete mu yevala no pululu.
> Sikileko! Sikileko vali!

4. At this, the hiding children whistle softly, so as not to immediately give away their hiding spots. Whether or not It manages to find someone, he sings the song again. After several songs, it's likely that he will find all of the players . . . especially if a few, tired of hiding, whistle a bit louder!

5. The first player caught becomes It in the next game.

KWANZAA

In this country, the holiday of Kwanzaa was developed by Maulana Karenga, chairman of the Black Studies Department at the California State University at Long Beach, in 1966. He conceived of the idea of African-Americans exploring the roots of their heritage and celebrating their achievements, with ceremonies centering on the family. The concept grew out of the renewed interest in the 1960s about African cultures. More than ever before in the United States, black Americans learned African languages, wore African clothing, adopted African customs and practices, and gave their children African names. Many colleges formed African-American Studies departments, and all across the country museums and other institutions were founded that were devoted to African art, culture, and history.

Another reason for introducing Kwanzaa was to reinforce values in the African-American community through promoting what Professor Karenga called Nguzo Saba or the "Seven Principles":

The Seven Principles:

Umoja : ("Unity") To be together — as a family, community, nation, and race.

Kujichagulia ("Self-Determination"): To decide your own future.

Ujima ("Collective Work and Responsibility"): To work together and be responsible for each other.

Ujamaa ("Cooperative Economics"): To operate your own shops, stores, and other businesses.

Nia ("Purpose"): To do what you can to make your people great.

Kuumba ("Creativity"): To do as much as you can to create beautiful and strong communities, and to improve existing communities.

Imani ("Faith"): To believe in yourself and your people.

These values, Professor Karenga wrote, were what "African-Americans needed in order to rebuild and strengthen family, community and culture and become a self-conscious social force in the struggle to control their destiny and daily life."

A third reason for Kwanzaa was essentially to provide people of African descent with an American-based holiday. In the 1960s Black History Month was not recognized on a national level as it is today, and it wasn't until the 1980s that Martin Luther King Jr. Day became a national holiday. Kwanzaa was designed to fill a gap — with the exceptions of Cinco de Mayo and Chinese New Year, holidays in the United States have European origins — and to focus specifically on African-American families.

In Africa the length of "first fruits" celebrations varied — some were three days, others were nine, and others were somewhere in between. Kwanzaa is observed for seven days, based on the Zulu tribe's celebrations and because each day is devoted to one of the Seven Principles. The dates of Kwanzaa are December 26 to January 1. Among the reasons for Professor Karenga's choosing these dates is that they would not conflict with the other major December holidays, Christmas and Hanukkah, and, more specifically, he wrote, Kwanzaa could be more quiet and family-oriented and not be influenced by "the high-priced hustle and bustle of Christmas buying and selling . . . [an] avoidance of the crass commercialism usually associated with this period and for savings on any modest gifts one might want to purchase in the context of Kwanzaa gift-giving guidelines."

Today, African-Americans have many reasons for celebrating Kwanzaa, including those first outlined by Professor Karenga. Most important is that this is a joyful holiday that encourages the participation of children with adult cooperation. If you haven't observed Kwanzaa before, perhaps this year will be the first of many celebrations.

CELEBRATING KWANZAA

Kwanzaa is only thirty years old, yet this family-oriented holiday has been embraced by millions of African-Americans.

Families (and schools) prepare for the holiday by decorating their homes with Kwanzaa symbols. A straw placemat called an *mkeka* (em-KAY-kah) is placed on a table. One ear of corn — called *muhindi* (moo-HIN-dee) — is placed on the mat for each child in the family. Often other fruits and vegetables are placed on the mat to represent the harvest. Collectively, the crops are called *mazao* (mah-ZAH-o).

Also part of the Kwanzaa celebration are handmade gifts called *zawadi* (zah-WAH-dee), which can be in the form of necklaces, dolls, beads, and other crafts. Many families include books of African folktales that can be read over the seven days to learn more about African ancestry. Crafts and books can be exchanged as gifts between youngsters and grownups.

In the center of the table is placed the *kinara* (kee-NAR-rah), a wooden candle holder with seven candles. In the center of the kinara is a black candle representing African skin. To the left are three red candles that represent struggles and endurance. To the right are three green candles representing hopes for a prosperous future.

Each day of Kwanzaa a candle is lit. Also, each day begins with the question *Habari gani* (hah-BAR-ee GAH-nee), or "What is the news?" This prompts the day's discussion and celebration among family members.

First Day: The black candle is lit to celebrate unity. The family is encouraged to relax together and discuss their thoughts and feelings about Kwanzaa.

Second Day: Light the red candle, representing self-determination. It is a day to teach African traditions and customs. Some families do this by learning how to play an African musical instrument, others by wearing traditional African clothing.

Third Day: A green candle, representing collective work and responsibility, is lit. As the principle indicates, this is a good day to take on a chore or task around the house — especially one that's been waiting awhile!

Fourth Day: Another red candle is lit, this one representing cooperative economics. Family members can purchase a gift they have been saving for, ones that the family can share.

Fifth Day: Light another green candle to represent purpose. Families use this day as an opportunity to think about the future and to establish goals, family ones and individual ones.

Sixth Day: Creativity is the day's theme, and the third red candle is lit. Family members invent dances, create projects, compose songs, write poems or stories.

Seventh Day: The third green candle, representing faith, is lit. Families focus on positive thoughts and view the future optimistically. While special meals may have been made all week, this day is one for a special feast called a *karamu* (kaa-RAH-moo). Roasted yams and collard greens are typical ingredients of the feast.

There is a ceremony part to the feast. It begins with an adult spilling a few drops of water from a cup designated as the *kikombe cha umoja* (kee-KOM-bay cha oo-MOE-jah) or family Kwanzaa cup, each drop representing African ancestors. The cup is then passed around, with everyone taking a sip. Thanks is then given for the food of the feast . . . and it's time to eat.

After the meal, it's time for music, especially the kind that people can dance and sing to. This is the happy ending to Kwanzaa.

KWANZAA ACTIVITIES

There are no specific "games" associated with Kwanzaa, yet there are enjoyable crafts and activities. We've included this section in the book because of the holiday's strong connection to Africa. Another reason is that although Kwanzaa occurs in December, many youngsters will find some of the activities entertaining at any time of year.

What is the origin of Kwanzaa? First, let's look at the holiday's roots in Africa. In many parts of Africa there were ceremonies to celebrate the beginning of the harvest season, with farmers giving thanks for crops that would become food. In the Swahili language, for example *Matunda ya Kwanze* means "first fruits." Records of these ceremonies date back as far as Ancient Egypt in the north (called Pert-In-Min) and in such other ancient African civilizations as Yorubaland and Ashantiland. In southern Africa the Zulu (Umkhosi), Matabele (Inxwala), Thonga (Luma), and Lovedu (Thegula) tribes also held harvest celebrations.

Whatever they were called and wherever they were held, the harvest celebrations were an occasion for people of a tribe or village to express gratitude for nature's gifts, in addition to acknowledge the hard work that was part of producing those gifts. Another important element was for people to be together, to reaffirm the bonds between them and the sense of community.

Kinara ▽

As explained above, a *kinara* is the display of seven candles. Materials are a flat piece of wood about a foot long, seven bottle caps, paint, aluminum foil, three green candles, three red candles, and one black candle.

1. Decorate the piece of wood with paint (optional).

2. Cut seven pieces of aluminum foil, each one about 6 inches square.

3. To form candle bases, place a bottle cap in the center of each piece of aluminum foil. Fold up the foil, leaving the edges loose enough so a candle can fit in.

4. In a straight line, glue the caps and foil covers onto the wood. Let the glue dry.

5. Put the black candle in the center holder, then the three red candles in the holders to the left, and finally the three green candles in the right-hand holders. Squeeze the aluminum foil around the candles.

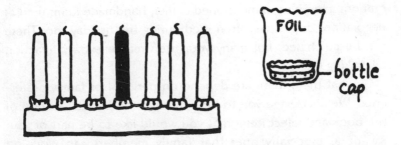

Mkeka ▼

This is a mat that was woven by hand, using straw, but here is how to make one from paper. Materials you'll need are scissors, glue, and red, green, and black construction paper (18 x12 inches).

1. Cut 12 strips of paper — 4 of each color — 18 inches long and 1 inch wide.

2. Alternating colors, place the strips of paper next to each other on a flat surface.

3. Cut 18 strips of paper — 6 of each color — 12 inches long and 1 inch wide.

4. To hold all the long strips together, glue one 12-inch strip along the edges of the 18-inch strips.

5. One by one, take the other 12-inch strips and weave them in, beginning next to the glued 12-inch strip. Go above and below next to the strip that you went below and above. Alternate colors, though you can create any pattern that pleases you.

6. Glue any loose edges. There's your *mkeka*!

The *kinara* and *mkeka* are necessary parts of the Kwanzaa celebrations. However, as mentioned earlier, handmade items used as decorations or gifts are often used during the holiday too. These can be purchased, but many youngsters realize extra satisfaction by making them.

What these items are depend on personal or family preference. We encourage you to look through the "Crafts" section of this book and select items that you would like to be part of your Kwanzaa, especially ones that family members can work on together.

Kikombe Cha Umoja ▼▼

This is the big cup that everyone drinks from as part of the Kwanzaa celebration. It represents the family living and working together.

The materials you will need are a cardboard tube (such as from a roll of paper towels or toilet paper), aluminum foil, a plastic egg (one that can be pulled apart), and tape.

1. Cut a 2-inch section from the cardboard tube. This will be the cup's stem.

2. Tape the tube to the small part of the plastic egg to form the base. Then tape the bigger part of the egg to be the cup itself.

3. Cover the entire cup, including base and stem, with aluminum foil. It will now resemble a metal cup.

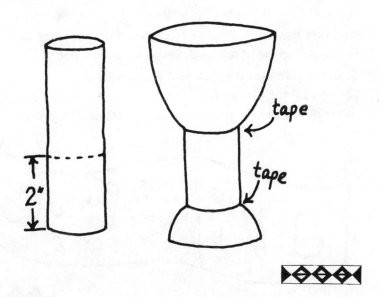

Mazao ▽

This is a "harvest banner" that represents the products of hard work. To create it, you will need a piece of paper or cloth of a light color, a long stick or thin pole, some yarn, paints that are the same colors of the fruits and/or vegetables you will use, and fruits and/or vegetables. The best ones to use are apples, oranges, pears, green peppers, and carrots.

1. With the help of an adult, cut slices of the fruits and vegetables. (Slice a carrot lengthwise.)

2. Take one side of each slice and paint its outer surface with a color that matches the fruit or vegetable. Then press the slice onto the paper or fabric.

3. Repeat this procedure until the banner is covered with painted impressions. You can use a paintbrush to add details, like seeds or stems, and to fill in spots where there isn't a full impression.

4. When the paper or fabric has dried, fold one edge of it over the stick, stapling or taping the edge to the banner.

5. Drape yarn over the stick too. If you wish to hang the banner, you can tie the two ends of a long piece of yarn to two ends of the stick and then use a thumbtack to attach the center of the yarn to a wall.

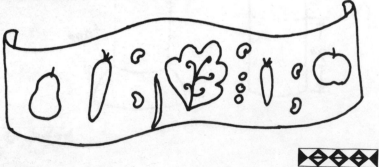

Candle Favors ▽

Children are often fascinated by the Kwanzaa candles, but it's not a good idea for them to play with them. Here's the next best thing.

To make these "candles" you will need cardboard toilet-tissue tubes, red and yellow tissue paper, scissors, glue, and red, green, and black construction paper. For the "treat," use nuts, raisins, and/or candy.

1. For each candle you're going to make, spread glue on a cardboard tube. Then wrap each tube with green, black, or red paper.

2. Scissor out a 10-inch square of tissue paper for each candle, using the two colors. Fold into the center of each piece the treat.

3. Wedge into one end of each tube the treat-containing tissue paper. The edges left hanging out should be crinkled a bit, 2 or 3 inches emerging.

4. Stand the candles up on their bases. They now resemble colorful burning candles. During the Kwanzaa celebration, these favors can be given to children who can pull out the "flame" and find their treats.

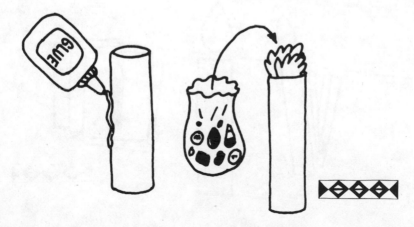

Candle Game ▼

Part of the fun of Kwanzaa is when families play games together. It's even more fun when you make your own game. Here is one example, for two players.

To create this game you will need scissors, glue, red, black, and green markers, construction paper (red, green, black, orange, and white), fourteen clothespins, and a shoe box.

1. Cut out fourteen flame shapes from a piece of orange construction paper.

2. From other pieces of construction paper, cut out six green, six red, and two black candles the same size and width as the clothespins.

3. Glue the candles to one side of each clothespin and then a flame shape atop each one. The tops of your candles should be the "handle" end, the end that doesn't attach to objects.

4. Cut from white construction paper fourteen "cards" about 2 inches square. With the markers, draw a black candle on two cards, a green candle on six cards, and a red candle on the remaining six cards.

HOW TO PLAY:

1. The players sit opposite each other with the shoe box between them. Each player receives one black, three green, and three red candles. Place the cards face down in the shoe box.

2. Players take turns picking up cards. Each card tells a player which candle should be attached to the (lengthwise) side of the box. As the candles are attached, they should be in the order of when they are lighted during Kwanzaa.

3. If a player cannot use a card — for example, you pick a green card and you have no more green candles left — It is placed back in the box.

4. A player wins who has attached all seven candles.

INDEX